CLAIRVOYANCY
The Truth

CLAIRVOYANCY
The Truth

Kris Sky

ROBERT HALE · LONDON

ISBN 0 7090 5019 4

Robert Hale Limited
Clerkenwell House
Clerkenwell Green
London EC1R 0HT

Photoset in Palatino by
Derek Doyle & Associates, Mold, Clwyd.
Printed by St Edmundsbury Press Ltd,
Bury St Edmunds, Suffolk.
Bound by WBC Bookbinders Ltd, Bridgend, Mid-Glamorgan.

Contents

Acknowledgements

This book is for the most part all my own work. No one has given me any interesting little pieces to be included and I've certainly not pinched, adapted, or adopted anyone else's ideas, thoughts, theories or philosophy. The method of using the tarot cards and the interpretation of them is completely and solely my own. What I have been lucky enough to use however, is the professional constructive advice of a Mr Steve Sands, who freely donated his time and talent in order to help produce a manuscript worthy of a publisher's appraisal. Thank you Steve, it appears that at last I've got it right, or should that be write?!

There are other special people who have contributed more towards my sanity than to the book. These people didn't assist me with the writing of the book but they did help me to live with the flipping thing. So here I go in print no less.

I must say thanks to Sue Burrows who encouraged me to go professional in the first place. There have been occasions when I have regretted this, but I'm glad to say that they were few and far between. Then there's Diane, a good friend who said, 'Go on, write about your experiences.' And Margaret, who had the awful task of reading the original manuscript, then the agony of telling me exactly what she thought of it. Correcting my atrocious spelling kept her in stitches for weeks. Thanks to my drinking partners, Val and Tom, who laughed at me and with me, taking the edge off the irritating days. I must take this opportunity to say a big thank you to my children, Sarah, Isobel, Christine and John Adam – for taking bookings, driving me, understanding me and just being great kids. I dare say that will cost me a fortune, but there it is. My many clients must not be forgotten. Without them none of this would have been possible. I sincerely hope that their experience with me has been constructive and enjoyable. Last but by no means least I have to thank my husband John. How he has managed to put up with my crazy ways I shall never know. He's always succeeded in keeping my feet on the floor, even when my head was in the clouds. The production of this book would have been much more difficult without his help, his consideration and his love.

Dedication

For Mum and Dad who never expected too much or too
little of me. Your love and care for me as a child had
magical and enchanting qualities that I now know to be a
most precious and rare gift. I will treasure the many happy
memories all of my life. Your imperfections only
succeeded in making you perfect.

Preface

Why does anyone write a book? Why should anyone, especially someone like me, even consider taking up pen and paper to struggle for months on end with spelling, diction, antiquated typewriters and impossible cantankerous word processors? The obvious answer is that I'm deranged, or vain in my belief that other people will be interested in what I've got to say. Well, I suppose since they say that there's a book in everyone, there had to be one in me. However, if anyone had told me six years ago that I could string the best part of 70,000 words together, I'd have told them that they were likely candidates for the local mental institute. For me even a postcard presents unlimited difficulties. So, why did I put this manuscript together? Not for all the usual reasons I can assure you. No! This book is not some lifelong ambition, nor a whimsical desire born in a moment of intuitive madness. Neither was it originally put together with the idea of fame or fortune. Not that I'd shun either, I could do with a little bit of extra cash. But then again, couldn't we all? This book, such as it is, had to be written and it had to be written by me. This was predicted over six years ago. With psychic vision I was permitted a rare glimpse into my own future. I actually saw myself walking down a street in Nottingham city centre. As I strolled past a fairly well-known bookshop I glanced into the window. There before me was my own face, emblazoned on the front of a book, surrounded by tarot cards. Below my face was the name, my name, Kris Sky. At the top of the picture it simply read, 'Clairvoyancy: The Truth'. This was my book and for some unknown reason I wasn't in the least bit surprised to find it there. I was still in two minds as to whether I liked the dust-cover or the photo of me on it, but that was just a bit of vanity creeping in. Still, we all have our own little foibles, and I had to look that word up in the dictionary.

So there you are. This book, and even the fact that you, the reader, should now peruse this preface, was all foreseen by me over six years ago. As soon as I knew that I was going to write a book and succeed in getting it published, I started to make notes on interesting cases that I had been involved with. I gathered any relevant material and stored it until it was time to blend it with my psychic knowledge and so produce the inevitable – this book! Wondering how to go about writing a preface, I decided to conduct my own survey. This revealed that most of my friends and business colleagues, even the very intelligent ones, never ever read a preface page. So since few of you are likely to read mine, I intend to keep it short and to the point.

Every word of this book was written by me in my very own original manner, with or without style. You will find in these pages, along with my thoughts and feelings, just a few of my many psychic deeds and actions. However, the main reason for this book is to help many people come to terms with psychic ability, whether it's within themselves or some other member of their family. Reading this book will, I hope, help you to understand exactly what true psychic power is capable of. Freed from the ritualistic claptrap that usually surrounds this subject, we can harness commonsense with psychic sense. For in truth, only together can both senses acquire their maximum potential. Then and only then, with both senses in harmony, will you discover the truly valuable qualities of psychic power.

'Every man has his own God, and no man has the right to destroy that God.'

Jack Denham

'You have to use your own eyes to see, your own heart to feel. No one can teach you to love or listen, to feel or see. No one can interpret your psychic visions.'

Psy

Introduction

In this ultra-modern day and age, the more sceptical of
you ask if there's a need for clairvoyant and psychic
people such as myself. You may believe that we, the
soothsayers of the past, have no right to trespass into your
safe black and white world, where facts are facts and
analytically proven or, unceremoniously ditched, scrap-
ped or just plain discarded. There are for you at least, no
grey areas. And yet! And yet! Even you the sceptic now
peruse these pages. Searching for what? Proof! Proof that
your scientific convictions are correct. After all, you've
had a lifetime to confirm those beliefs, haven't you? And
yet, and yet ... You know that it's been proved that we
only use about one-fifth of the brain's capacity, so what's
the rest of it there for? What is the rest of our sophisticated
brain supposed to be used for? What mysterious, glorious,
and as yet, unidentified powers lurk beneath the surface
of this ingenious organ?

I don't claim to have all the answers, I don't even
know half the questions. But I do feel there are many
people who have unknowingly used some of those
powers. Somehow they have managed to tune into that
uncharted part of the brain and produced the impossible
and the unbelievable. These people are the visionaries,
seers, healers, mediums, clairvoyants and psychics. The
evidence is clearly there for all to see, if they really want
to. It's not even in cryptic form for it's only superficial
beliefs that place the proof of the existence of psychic
power just out of reach. The ridiculous part about this is
we actually prefer to believe devils and demons are
capable of capturing our minds and hearts. Because
psychic power cannot easily be explained, it's frequently

classed as a gift from the devil rather than a fantastic talent or a very natural ability that dwells deep within every brain.

Let's look at the everyday written historical evidence. Poor Joan of Arc for instance heard voices – not that it did her a lot of good. First of all it was thought that she was mental. Then many believed that she had a direct line to God. Eventually the poor sod was burnt at the stake as a witch. On how the mighty do fall! After much soul searching however, the church did correct their mistake and make her a saint. Not that that did her much good either.

Leonardo da Vinci was a visionary, as his paintings prove, and he too must have taken some stick for his beliefs. His sketches of aircraft in 1488 prove beyond a shadow of a doubt that he knew even then that man would one day fly. This couldn't have been pure luck as there's far too much detail in his pictures for that. Somehow the psychic side of his brain must have propelled him forward in time and revealed to him the aircraft of today.

Our own Bible is riddled with prophecies, predictions, healers and the occasional miracle worker. Jesus's own birth was well and truly predicted. Joseph was told by an angel that his wife would soon give birth to the son of God. (The consequences of that statement would have brought about a very different reaction today.) And three wise men didn't follow a star as training for the local marathon. The ten commandments weren't delivered by post and Noah wasn't into keeping up with the Joneses when he built his boat. As we all know, the list is endless. Psychic ability in action is described, rigorously vetted and meticulously logged in the Bible and countless history books for all to see, and yet, many still deny its existence.

I predict that the 1990s are going to be the years of greater understanding. All types of psychic abilities and religious beliefs will be examined and if not understood at least tolerated. No longer will true psychics deny and hide their skill through fear of being ridiculed or scorned. The churches and its followers will have to come to terms with the fact that the psychics of today and even yesterday are not evil and do not deal with the devil. Psychic ability in its many forms is a skill and a talent like any other, not a gift from the devil.

There has always been a need for clairvoyants, healers and psychics and there always will be. If we weren't needed you can be sure that we wouldn't be here.

1   Family History

In order to understand psychic power and indeed psychic people, such as myself, it will be necessary for you to step back in time with me. This will enable us to sweep aside the mountain of written information which far from supplying the public with facts merely provides us with myths and often downright lies. Together we will dispose of much of the garbage that has surrounded the subject with a cloak of mystery since time immemorial. First and foremost let's dispose of the myth that all clairvoyants have hard lives, weird childhoods or are unloved. This is certainly not true of my past.

April 1947, the year of the great freeze. Snow fell continuously for days on end. People were entombed in their own homes and the snow-covered roads became treacherous and impassable. Abandoned cars and lorries were quickly and quietly covered with a cold white blanket of snow, rendering them invisible to the naked eye. The whole of Britain had come to a standstill, most of the country gripped in the icy fingers of despair. Only a few, mainly the wealthy, could afford to appreciate the Christmas card scenery that was to be seen from every door and window. Workers everywhere were worried about fuel, food and relatives or friends they had been unable to contact. Our house was no different, except for one small fact. My impending and untimely arrival. Not that I wasn't wanted, or so I'm told. Just that Mum must have had enough to do keeping the house warm, the food hot and the family dry without having to drop everything to give birth to a four and a half pound mite. One who was eventually destined to try her patience to the limit and break her heart more times than I now care to remember.

A lesser woman with more foresight could have been forgiven if she had cast that same troublesome mite out into the cold, cold snow. Luckily for me, Mum was a strong, loving woman with, at that time, little or no foresight. I remember nothing of my birth, and have no desire to do so, unlike some who claim to recall every minute and gory detail. And even the early years escape this selective memory of mine, a memory that teachers, friends and family alike have compared to that of a cullender – one with the uncanny knack of straining away the vital juices and retaining the rubbish! It's now necessary for me to skip the first few years of my history and continue with the story at a later date of which I have an acceptable, if not total, amount of recall.

Both of my parents were great, although I must admit that as a child I was extremely close to my father. My love and trust in him was so great, at times, it must have been difficult for him to live up to my expectations. But he did, and he did it well. I was very proud of my dad. He was a very handsome man, even in other people's eyes. To me he appeared to be seven feet tall, but in truth, he was only five foot eight. His hair, like mine, was very dark, thick and wavy and his eyes were a deep shade of brown. His nose was slightly bent due to the fact that he had been a boxer in his younger days and it had been broken on two or three occasions. I often used to brag to my school friends that my dad had been a champion boxer, which indeed he had, though maybe not as grand as I had painted him. He seemed younger than most of my friends' dads, always having time for a game of football or swimming with the kids. In the summer months he would gather all the children on the street and take them to a nearby dyke. Once there he would promptly dam it up so that we could paddle in the ever deepening water. There were often times when I would sulk because he was paying too much attention to the other children but he would simply take me in his warm, strong arms and remind me that I was his little girl and I belonged to him. This special treatment usually did the trick. Then this truly spoilt brat would return to play with the rest of the kids, leaving Dad to sleep peacefully on the bank.

Dad was a miner, working most of his life at a pit in Bilsthorpe. I grew to hate that pit, always afraid that it would one day steal my precious father from me. There were so many accidents in those days. Dad, like many of his work-mates, spent many a day encased in plaster of Paris. When he was unable to get upstairs, his bed would be set up in the front room. There he would watch the television and moan about the skin itching beneath the plaster. One of the kids would often take a long, thin, steel knitting needle from Mum's knitting basket and then force it down the plaster to relieve the irritation. These sort of circumstances and events were frequent and I guess there must have been a lot of tension between Mum and Dad, but they never showed it. All we ever saw as children was a very loving couple, even when they were very short of money. My mother was fantastic and how she ever put up with me I will never know, for like a lot of young women, I was more than a handful.

Five feet of dynamite with natural red hair was how we used to describe Mum. She was a trim, prim woman, always smart and clean. Every week, without fail, she would briskly walk to the hairdressers where her short red locks would be washed and set in her usual style. Mum was never one to experiment. High-heeled shoes were her one and only weakness. She loved pretty, delicate shoes. This was one vice she could afford because she had tiny feet, a petite size three. A little shop in the centre of Arnold where we lived used to supply her with all the size three samples her heart desired, at a greatly reduced price. Though she was small she walked like a model, with her back straight and her head held high. When walking with her, I could barely hear the short sharp tap of her heels because she was so light on her feet. She tried to teach me to walk the way she did. First of all I wore small Cuban heels, then as the years went by the size of the heel was increased. I often used to borrow her best shoes without asking, especially if I was going out to a new youth club or dance. But she'd know and would drop little sarcastic comments such as, 'You can always tell when someone inexperienced has been wearing high-heeled shoes because they twist the instep.' Message understood Mum, till next time. Other mums may not have understood their children, but mine did. She knew what I was thinking or doing ten minutes before I did. Looking back, I believe she must also have been psychic.

She laid down the law in our house which was just as well, because had it been left to Dad we would have got away with blue murder. I can't say she ruled with a rod of iron, but if she said do something, we did it. Although she never hit any of us she was a great shot with her slippers. I'll explain. If one of us had angered Mum and were trying to escape her exceptionally sharp tongue, she would grab her slipper from her foot and throw it. Usually it hit the wall at a great rate of knots, then land with a splat at the offender's feet. This generally created enough effect to freeze the guilty party to the spot, whereupon Mum would continue her scolding with renewed ferocity and render us with the age old warning that we were not too big for a good hiding! I remember one particular occasion when a friend of mine, also called Chris, copped for a shot that was meant for me. Luckily Mum wore soft slippers so there was no damage, just a very apologetic, red-faced Mum. We all dearly loved Mum; she had an uncanny knack of making everything look easy. She was a great cook and even when times were hard we never noticeably went without. She thought nothing of baking her own bread and pastry. Her stew and dumplings were so delicious friends would suddenly appear from nowhere for dinner. Neighbours used to ask her for samples of her blackberry or raspberry vinegar and she even made her own ginger beer. Nothing ever seemed too much for her. She taught me to knit and sew but gave up on me when I tried to crochet and tat lace.

Mum was quite a jealous person and no woman in her right mind would try to get too close to Dad whilst she was about. However, far from annoying Dad, I think he actually encouraged a display of her possessiveness. Then, when her crystal green eyes were flashing in anger, he would tell her she was beautiful and he loved her, and he didn't care a cow who was listening. This he knew would cause her even more embarrassment. She would blush bright scarlet then turn on him and say, 'Jack you're impossible.' With that she would storm off in the opposite direction.

I was lucky enough to have two brothers and two sisters. My brother John was four years older than me. We got on very well. I loved him and followed him all over the place. This was quite all right until he reached the macho age of sixteen. Suddenly he wanted to be with his mates, his bikes and his girlfriends. I was left behind and boy, did I kick up a stink. I frequently chased away his many girlfriends. Once I even gave one of them my pet ferret to hold, knowing full well she was petrified. I tried to hang around his bikes, and talked Triumph, Beezer and Norton with the best. All to no avail, it was useless. All they wanted me for was to mash their tea and occasionally, if I was very good, I was bestowed the great honour of being allowed to polish their precious bikes. Eventually I took the hint, found myself other friends and left brother John to get on with his life.

My sister Ann is two years younger than I am. We used to fight quite a lot as we had very different personalities. Ann was quiet and very shy, with fair hair and blue eyes. She was a little bit bigger than me and when we did fight she usually won. Even though we were not close there must have been some sort of bond because whenever there was any trouble at school, or with friends on the road, we would stick together like glue. I know we are closer now than we have ever been. I'm glad that, as we've grown older, we've been able to understand each other better.

Joe, my younger brother, is almost a replica of John. He's about average build with very dark brown hair and eyes. Joe was very fond of Ann. They were almost inseparable. Even at the tender age of ten Joe was a worker. He loved to earn money. He scraped snow from paths and gathered watercress from streams. He'd also shop for OAP's and for a small charge would tackle any job set for him. It was impossible for anyone to dislike Joe. His cheeky face and lovable ways made him a favourite with everyone.

Dorothy, the baby of the family, was a pretty, slim, blue-eyed child. She had straight, almost white hair and was an incredible minx. She was forever in the most amazing trouble. She climbed trees like a monkey. On one occasion she cut the hair of every child on the road with Dad's barber's shears. She left many of them with some sort of Mohican hair style and shaved a two inch parting through the hair of others. Another time she put a full packet of soap powder into Mum's copper boiler just to see what would happen. Needless to say, soap-suds covered the floor of the wash-house and then ran down the steps into the street, much to the amusement of friends and neighbours. Dorothy really was a scamp, but a lovable scamp. She certainly put a lot of fun, spice and love into our lives.

So now you know that this psychic at least had a happy life. No beatings – only the occasional clip around the ear. No separated parents, or weird upbringing. Just a happy, normal family life complete with its ups and downs – and I wouldn't change one minute of it for all the money in the world!

2 Realization

We are all born with some degree of psychic sense. For many years it remains dormant, like a seed in the ground waiting for the sun and rain to stimulate its growth. No one knows for certain what triggers off psychic ability. There's no set time, place or person that will suddenly develop psychic insight. I believe psychic power is activated by a need, a vital need in ourselves.

The psychic seed has to be strong, very strong, if it is to survive the first few ignorant years. All too often the germ of psychic sense is smothered by the much stronger commonsense. Once psychic sense is aroused, like any other talent that we inherit, it will need careful nurturing if it's to develop into a valuable asset. Too much, too little, or the wrong type of information can corrupt and stifle what should be a most treasured gift.

I now believe claustrophobia triggered off my psychic ability. At the time I don't think I even knew that I was claustrophobic. What I did know, was that even at the tender age of eleven, I hated classrooms full of children. I detested lifts and crowds. Being locked in any room, large or small, almost drove me crazy.

I tried to understand why these situations worried me. Commonsense told me there was nothing to worry about, and yet psychic sense was telling me I was in the wrong environment. I rebelled against teachers who tried to keep me in crowded, overbearing classes. I often found myself, as they said, day-dreaming. Really I was escaping not only from the place, but from the time, where I felt a prisoner. I had to escape. I had to be free, mentally if not physically. Away from the walls or the situation that smothered and entombed me. It was in these day-dreaming moments, as I watched the clouds in the sky through the high classroom windows, I would dream of my home, just like any other kid I suppose. The only difference was that I would know what was for dinner and I would know exactly what else was waiting for me when I got home.

Once, as I sat watching the clouds go by, my father's face seemed to appear within them. At first I remember thinking that it was just as amusing trick of my imagination, a coincidence. Then my heart started to race and I felt sick because I knew something was wrong, terribly wrong and I had to get home. There was no reasoning with this sensation, just panic. I ran out of the class saying I was going to be sick. The teacher, who had a very sensitive stomach, was only too pleased to let me go.

I ran out of the school, across the playground and past the girls' toilet block where I was supposed to be going. It was a good twenty minutes walk to my home, but my feet flew down roads and across fields. My heart beat faster and faster from the running and also from fear of what would be waiting for me when I finally reached home. I should have known. I'd seen it all too often many times before. There at the window was Mum, waiting, not for me I hasten to add. Oh no, she wasn't at all curious as to why I had suddenly appeared out of the blue. She was watching for the dreaded black pit ambulance which she knew would yet again bring my father home. Her pretty face would age by the minute and her tidy red hair would seem to lose its shine as she ran her fingers through it. As she paced back and forth I could feel the pain that tortured her mind and body but I wasn't old enough to console her. Only wise enough not to try.

Mum was psychic, although she would never ever admit to it. She often knew Dad was in some sort of danger, sometimes even before he went to work. She would never say that Dad had been involved in an accident until he actually turned up in the ambulance. I think in her mind, predicting an accident brought it about. So she kept her thoughts to herself.

The ambulance arrived and all the curtains on the street moved. Women watched until it stopped outside our house. Mum was already on the road waiting for the men to open the back doors of the van. Neighbours appeared on the doorsteps ready to assist if they were needed, even if it was only to make a cup of tea. The relief on Mum's face was apparent even at this stage. She knew that if Dad were conscious he would have insisted on being taken home before he would go on to the hospital. He always did this, no matter how much the ambulance men complained and said they would lose their jobs. Dad would create until they took him home and then Mum would join him in the ambulance. She used to tell him off as well, saying it was more important for him to get medical attention than to worry about her worrying. But I don't think he took any notice of her either.

3   Pit Props

The first serious psychic experience I had occurred when I was about ten years old. I'd skived off school knowing full well that because my father had been on the night-shift he would have to return to the pit that morning if he wanted to get his wages. I had every intention of going with him. He wasn't keen on taking me. I was one of the world's worst travellers, especially on buses. However, I begged to go with him, promised not to be sick and vowed to be good. After much deliberation on his part, it worked and I was allowed to accompany him.

It was a long walk to the bus stop. My little legs welcomed the opportunity to rest, even on the hard uncomfortable bus seats. We sat upstairs on the bus because Dad, like a lot of miners, liked to smoke.

The old bus trundled along, picking up men with tired, worn faces who were about to go on the afternoon shift. As the bus filled, the air became thick with smoke. So, promise or no promise, I started to feel sick. As we were only a few minutes into a forty minute journey Dad was far from amused. After opening a window, much to the disgust of the other passengers, Dad told me to take deep breaths of the cool air. Then he produced a packet of barley sugar sweets from his pocket. These, he assured me, would stop even the worst form of travel sickness. It worked; I soon felt much better. When I look back on this incident now, I think Dad must have been some sort of hypnotist. He certainly had a way with words.

I managed to complete the journey without any major mishaps, but I was still glad to get off that bus. The wages office was quite a long way from where the bus had dropped us, but I didn't mind. I enjoyed listening to the men as they marched in their heavy boots to the canteen or the wages shed. Every so often one of the men would say how pretty I was and I would absolutely glow. I loved to be complimented. And tramping along with the men I had a captive, albeit moving, audience. Miners very rarely swore in the presence of women or children. As children we were expected to be seen and not heard, and only to speak in adult company when we were spoken to. These were not written rules, just a way of life where men were men with dirty, dangerous jobs to do, but they respected the women in their lives. These same women, far from being insulted or demanding sexual equality, just got on with life. They knew that their job of keeping the family together was all important.

On our way to the wages office, we had to pass the timber yard. This was where all the pit props were stored until they were needed in the mine. We passed one stack after another, all the same distance apart, all the same frightening height and colour. These enormous brown mountains of wood made my head spin. I felt as if they were getting bigger and bigger while I was actually shrinking. This feeling or impression disturbed me enough to cause me to seek the security of my father's hand. Which, at that brief moment was just out of reach. I turned to see my father disappearing into the maze of wood. He called to me as his pace slowed. I started to run to catch up with him.

'Hurry up gal,' he shouted, 'we'll be late.'

I stood there, and immediately froze to the spot, whilst he took two, maybe even three more steps into the timber yard. 'Come on,' he said, this time more impatiently. I hesitated, I wanted to go to him. I needed him but my feet wouldn't move. He stood there, a man I'd move heaven and earth for, but I could not, would not, follow him. As I stood there, the great tree trunks that had towered above my dad's head, started to fall with strange jerking movements. I panicked, my heart stopped, and I screamed, 'Dad, Dad,' until panic or fear robbed me of my voice, my legs and my consciousness.

The next thing I knew, Dad was picking me up, and dusting me down.

'What the hell's a matter with you? What are you playing at? If this is the way you're going to act, you won't come again my lass.' Dad was angry and worried. The stones and gravel had cut into my legs. My eyes were stinging with hot salty tears and my head spun with confusion. None of that mattered because Dad was safe. He was there with me, and that was all that mattered.

Men who had walked with us now advised Dad, saying, 'Clip her round the ear Jack' or 'Give her a good hiding'. Dad was more concerned about the blood that now poured from my leg. I still could not believe that the pit props had not fallen. I turned round and round in disbelief, expecting to find what I had seen behind me, but it wasn't there. Dusted down and calmed, we started off again on our journey to the wages shed. Only this time I persuaded Dad to walk all the way around the timber yard. He was not amused, but anything was better than having an hysterical ten-year-old on his hands.

I spent the rest of the day being the most perfect little girl you could imagine. We went to a friend's house for a cup of tea and there I sat, quiet and still, whilst pit business was discussed. The two men obviously had many friends with whom they had shared some interesting and amusing past escapades. Neither could resist the opportunity to reminisce.

A photo was retrieved from a sideboard that looked large enough to play in. The picture was a group of people who were admiring an antique charabanc. It was clear even to me that most of the men in that group were a lot older than the two men who now studied the picture. There was some confusion as to who on the picture was still alive and who had, in fact, passed on. Dad informed his friend David that he knew for certain that two of the men in the picture were no longer with us.

'I wonder if old George is still alive,' said a voice just behind us. It was David's wife. She was pretty with tight, curly blonde hair, which I thought was absolutely beautiful. She went on. 'He lived near us years ago. We used to treat him like a grandfather. Then because his health was failing, they bought a bungalow near the sea. We always said that we would go and see them, but you know what it's like. We never got round to it, and I'll bet it's too late now.' She now looked quite sad, obviously feeling a little guilty that she had not found the time, or made the effort, to visit her old friend.

Dad then did a very strange thing. He took a hair from my long dark locks and asked the lady of the house for her wedding ring. The hair was then passed through the ring and suspended above the head of a man in the photograph. I sat there fascinated, glued to the chair, I wasn't the only one. David and his wife were also intrigued.

'This man is still with us,' Dad said, much to the relief of all who were watching.

The ring was then suspended over the head of another man. This time the ring swung back and forth.

'I'm sorry to say, this one has passed on.'

Even though none of them knew the poor old gentleman, a sort of depression filled the air. The process was repeated again and again, until all the men in the picture had been covered. Sometimes David was able to confirm that Dad's statement was in fact true as he appeared to know more about the men in the picture than Dad. Some, much to my bitter disappointment, were to remain a mystery. However, once again, my father had proved to be a marvel to me, which he continued to be for the rest of his life.

We all finished our tea and went off to the miners' welfare. I was given my pop and Dad had his pint and game of cards. Every so often one of Dad's mates would remind him of the so-called tantrum that I had thrown in the timber yard. Then they would laugh at me saying, 'Don't be daft lass. Them pit props have been stored like that for years. There ain't no way they'd fall.'

Dad just brushed their comments to one side, saying I was born with an overactive imagination. He was like that, never one to harp on about past events. As far as he was concerned it was over and done with, so the day ended happily.

Mum must have been told what had happened that day, because she asked me why I had performed, as she called it. I needed to tell her. She was a good listener and I

expected her to be able to explain why I had seen such a
terrible thing. Recalling the vision was painful. Mum
sensed my anguish and told me not to worry, that I had
once again been day-dreaming. I don't think I quite
believed her, but I was happy to accept her explanation.

Six days later as I scanned the paper for information on
the night's television programmes I found my eyes drawn
to a story of a pit disaster. Not just any pit, but Bilsthorpe.
This accident had not happened below ground as they
usually do, but above ground, in the timber yard. Tears
filled my eyes and I felt cold and sick. Three people had
been killed. Pit props that had been so safely stacked for
so many years had quite inexplicable fallen.

I looked at the happy smiling faces of the young office
girl and the two men involved and cried. Somehow I felt
responsible for their deaths. I knew that I had seen those
damned pit props fall, a whole week before. I thought that
if I'd told someone, convinced someone, then they could
have prevented it. My parents gently but firmly told me it
was only a coincidence. When other people commented
on my strange experience in the timber yard they were
quickly hushed up. Neither Mum nor Dad wanted their
daughter to grow up with the strange idea that she could
see into the future.

As the years passed, there were many such 'coinci-
dences'. I soon realized that it was best to keep some
things to myself. When I slipped up and started to tell
Mum about the dream that I'd had the previous night, she
would stop me, saying, 'Monday's dream, Tuesday
foretold, will always come true, no matter how old'.

It took me years to realize that this rhyme would fit any
day of the week, i.e., Wednesday's dream, Thursday
foretold, and so on. Mum knew I was different, but even
to this day, she considers this psychic business a load of
old rubbish. And it was certainly not to be encouraged in a
young child. Mum would patiently explain that dreams
were just dreams, usually brought on by watching too
much television or a vivid imagination. I remember one
occasion when we stood together at the kitchen sink
scraping the new potatoes for Sunday dinner. I told her of
the strange dream that I'd had the night before. In the

dream I had been holding a baby which had made Mum laugh.

'You nursing a baby, that will be the day madam!' She was well aware that I was not in the least bit interested in children. I always found them a little too smelly and a lot too noisy. I continued with the story.

'In this dream, I carried the baby up many, many stairs. The child was wrapped in a soft blue shawl. There was this awful smell that I couldn't quite recognize.' (I know, most people don't get odours in dreams, but I do!) 'Then the baby was taken from me by loving, warm, yet invisible arms. I willingly gave up the child, somehow knowing that it would be safe. Then once again I found the stairs and continued my journey, this time downwards. I hesitated on the last step, still cradling the pretty blue shawl that the baby had been wrapped in. I turned and saw a bin, then I carefully folded the shawl and dropped it into the container.'

Mum dropped the potato she had finished peeling into the saucepan, then she picked up two more and promptly put one firmly into my hand.

'Kris' she said, 'if you spend as much time working as you do dreaming, not only will we have potatoes for dinner, but you should end up a wealthy woman! I agree that it's strange, you dreaming of children, but that's all, lass. Dreams are often strange, but that's all they are, dreams. Now let's get on with the dinner before your dad gets home.'

The topic of conversation now moved to much more important issues. Such as, was the oven hot enough now for the Yorkshire puddings, and would we be needing the raspberry vinegar or the jam with them. The silly dream was swept away from my mind amidst the hustle and bustle of helping to prepare the all-important, ritualistic Sunday dinner for seven.

Three days later Mum was talking to Auntie Kath, who was looking quite pale and tired. Auntie Kath had rushed her youngest child to hospital in the middle of the night. The lifts were out of order, so she had had to walk up one flight of stairs after another.

Then she said, 'The beautiful new blue shawl that baby

had been wrapped in was ruined. I had to throw it in a hospital bin.' Mum looked at me then back at Kath.

'The baby's all right though, isn't he, Kath?' Mum sounded concerned.

'Yes, he's going to be fine now I'm glad to say,' was Kath's reply.

I left the women to continue with their conversation. I knew it would have been unwise to recall the dream I had had three days previously. As soon as Auntie Kath had said hospital, I had remembered the odour in the dream. It was obvious now. The lifts being out of order explained why I had walked up so many stairs. The blue shawl didn't need explaining. Once again, in the realm of dreams, I had stepped into the future. How or why I had been able to do so was to remain a mystery to me for many years to come.

4   After School

I was more than glad to leave school at fifteen. The advice offered by the careers officer was a complete waste of time. I told him, if it were possible, I wanted to work out of doors with animals. He told me not to be so daft and gave me a card. This arranged an interview for me at the local factory that made shirts and socks. For six solid weeks I mended thousands of new socks. Long ones, short ones, black, blue and green socks. I was bored daft, I was seeing socks in my dreams. It got too much for me, I gave in my notice, and swore I would never mend another sock as long as I lived. To this day socks that need mending get thrown straight into the dustbin.

I started work as a waitress and thoroughly enjoyed meeting people. The uniform , such as it was, was very flattering. A white blouse and a tight black skirt were the order of the day. And would you believe – we were actually encouraged to wear stiletto heels? I loved the uniform and the job. I could cope with any customer, young, old, grumpy or pleasant. The wages were pathetic, about two shillings an hour but the tips were great. I often earned more in tips than in wages. As a trained waitress, it was easy to drop in and out of jobs and it was in one of these jobs that I had yet another psychic experience.

My friend Christine and I had applied for work at the new local Wimpy bar which were all the rage then. Chris got the job as cook, and I was employed as a waitress. We were both asked to go in the day before the grand opening to help clean up. Since we were both broke, we were only too pleased to be given the opportunity to earn extra cash.

In the shiny new kitchen we found a waste disposal unit, nothing unusual today but we had never seen anything like it. To us this was space-age technology. Four of us stood around the sink feeding it with potato peelings, onion skins and bread. The strange new machine gurgled and growled and we were all fascinated – it even *sounded* hungry. Suddenly a tie being worn by one of the young lads swung over the sink as he leant over. The old woman who had been employed to wash the pots grabbed it and threatened to put it in the waste unit whilst he was still wearing it, if he walked over her clean floor again. We all laughed – the old gal had had us in stitches all morning with her jokes and her chasing the young chefs around with her mop. There was no danger of the tie being fed into the machine, but it triggered off a red alert in my head. I pressed all three of them up to the sink unit. I didn't want them to move backwards. They had to stay where they were. I was only a slip of a lass of about seven stone then and not very strong. They protested and told me to 'stop mucking about'. I didn't know what I was waiting for, but I knew they had to stay put. I had just about lost the battle when the electric box on the wall behind us exploded with an almighty bang. Flames and thick smoke filled the small kitchen. I was too frightened to be of any use, but a young ginger-haired lad grabbed a handy fire extinguisher and quickly dealt with the fire.

We were all in a state of shock, but that quickly passed. Soon we all pitched in to help clean the now smoke-stained walls and floor. The kitchen still had to be ready for the next day and we had to work fast, because now there was no electricity and the night was drawing in. When we had done all that we could, we sat in the empty, plush, and somewhat dark restaurant, to discuss the day's melo-drama. The little ginger-haired lad who had been so brave with the fire extinguisher was declared the hero of the day, which only succeeded in making him blush and stutter. As if to avoid any more talk of his heroics, he quickly turned the conversation to my direction.

'My God Kris, I don't know what you were mucking about at when you tried to push us into the sink, but I'm bloody glad you did. Any one of us could have been hurt, electrocuted even, had we been nearer that wall. God, weren't we lucky?'

I agreed with him, we all agreed with him. There was no point in telling them that I had been well aware that something was going to happen. After all, I didn't want them to think I was crazy. In those days people who thought they could see into the future and were daft enough to declare it were classed as mental by the majority. This was a fate I did not wish to share!

5 Omens

One would naturally assume that if a person has so much psychic sense, they would also have enough common-sense to use the talent that they were born with but this is not so. Take it from one who knows. When I reached the grand old age of nineteen, I rebelled against my psychic powers. I ignored them and even denied they existed, and why? Because I was madly and passionately in LOVE. His name was Ken, and to me he was the best thing since sliced bread. He was almost six feet tall, had blonde hair and beautiful blue eyes. More important than that, he was a professional singer and doing quite well at the time.

I was working as a petrol pump attendant when I met Ken. He tried to chat me up whilst I filled his car with petrol. I refused his offer of a night out, due to the fact that it was my birthday that day, and I had promised to go out with my mum and dad. Ken must have waited just out of sight for the rest of the day because when I finished work he was there offering me not only a lift home, but a lovely bouquet of flowers. I was spellbound; I think it must have been the first bouquet I had ever had. Needless to say we were soon going out together. He showered me with gifts, and frequently took me to the posh nightclubs where he worked.

His charm was irresistible, not only to me, but to the many people we met in clubland. It came as no surprise to my father when Ken, with all the decorum of a Victorian gentleman, asked Dad for my hand in marriage. Dad said if it was what I really wanted, then that was OK with him. Soon the fuss and bother of planning the perfect wedding was all about us.

Any doubts hovering at the back of my mind that this

could be anything less than a perfect match were smothered by my infatuation with and my overwhelming love and devotion for Ken.

When the psychic side of the brain is ignored, something rather bizarre starts to happen. Omens suddenly appear from out of every nook and cranny around you. Funny little things start to happen, which you casually toss to one side saying, 'superstitious nonsense' or 'old wives' tales'. Then there's 'claptrap', 'rubbish', and my all time favourite, *'coincidence'*.

These omens surrounded me and inundated me with bad luck symbols from the moment the wedding was announced. Since I refused to listen to the psychic side of my brain, and because I had ignored its power, it had to get to me another way. The only way it could warn me that I was making a great mistake was by using not only the people who were around me but also, quite cleverly, by using their deep primitive instincts. It was almost as if the psychic side of me was able to reach out and touch the minds of my friends. Then, even more impossible to believe, use them and even inanimate objects to produce what seemed like 101 foreboding omens.

Let me tell you about the first omen. Mum and I had gone to a lot of trouble to bake a three tier wedding cake. It was, I admit, a little ambitious, but we followed the recipe with precision, and as I have said before, there's not much Mum couldn't do when she tried. The cake was correctly stored, in three separate tins, until it was time to marzipan it. Then it was returned to its storage place until it was time for the first coat of icing. We had decided that since neither of us had a great deal of artistic talent, we would keep the cake stylish but simple and use bought decorations.

It looked great with its silver trimmings and pillars, as good as any we could buy in a shop, and a lot cheaper. We were really chuffed with ourselves, until the day before the wedding, when omen number one decided to rear its ugly head.

Mum put the three cakes on the table. They had all been covered with loose-fitting biscuit tins after we had finished the final icing, to protect them from dust and eager children's fingers. She carefully removed the first tim from the top and smallest cake.

'Oh my God, what on earth's happened?' said Mum. Her face was a picture of horror, as she snatched the tins from the remaining cakes. They all looked as though they had been used as culture slides to grow fungus on in a laboratory. The beautiful pure white icing was now covered in pink, grey, brown and yellow blotches. Mum sat down. I was close to tears. What the hell were we going to do? All our hard work had gone down the drain. There was no way it could be repaired in time for the wedding the next day. After much panic and rushing around, a cake was acquired from a local baker who just happened to have one almost ready. He very kindly informed us that the reason our cake had developed the dreaded lurgy was because we had not put on a thick enough layer of marzipan. All that had happened was that the juice of the dried fruit had seeped through and stained the icing. Needless to say the cake was still edible, and the kids loved it, and much to our surprise they thought the spotty cake was better than the white one. Yes, number one was a corker, and this as it happens, was just the beginning. There was much more to come!

Omen number two (sounds like a film sequel doesn't it?) was almost as bad as number one. Ken was encouraged to have a stag night. Now since he was almost teetotal, it wasn't quite his type of thing, but he went along with what the rest wanted. I had a quiet hen night out with my mum, my sisters and a few good friends. We returned home fairly early as we all needed a good night's sleep to recover from the episode with the cake. The men returned home a little later, with, much to my mum's disgust, Ken!

Mum ushered me upstairs out of the way saying, 'He can't see the bride, it's bad luck. I tell you, *bad luck.*'

I did as she said, but Ken kept shouting for me. Eventually I could stand it no longer, I had to find out what the idiot was ranting and raving about. Have you ever seen a six foot, teetotaller when he's had about six pints? Suddenly he's reduced to a three foot, jibbering idiot. Not a pretty sight. He could hardly stand, his hair was a mess and he certainly couldn't string three words together. Which resulted in him getting very frustrated and eventually trying to take a swing at me with his fist. His fist missed my faces by inches and hit the wall behind. All the skin from his knuckles was left on the rough wall. Blood poured from the wound, and I stood there frightened to death. My brother finally came to the rescue and dragged a very apologetic Ken into the kitchen. There Mum tried to bathe the hand and sober him up with black coffee.

Mum was fuming and kept saying, 'I told you it would bring bad luck if you saw him. He should have gone straight home.'

Oh boy, was she mad! Poor Ken sat there drunk and bewildered in a kitchen that looked more like a bridal shop. Mum had managed to cover my bridal gown with a sheet. There was no way he was going to see that. But the six rainbow-coloured bridesmaid dresses were stretched full length across the large kitchen table. Ken said how pretty they were, and he hadn't realized that it was going to be a rainbow wedding. Even in that alcoholic state he was still able to use his charm, telling Mum and I how fantastic we were to make such lovely dresses. The spell didn't last long. (You've guessed it, maybe you're psychic.) He stood up to kiss me and knocked his coffee over with such force that all six bridesmaid dresses were splattered with black coffee. They were now an ideal match for the spotty wedding cake, which was more than Ken was for Mum. I rushed him out of the kitchen and he didn't protest. Even in that state he knew that he stood a better chance of surviving twenty rounds with Mohammed Ali than one round with my mum at that moment.

Mum washed, dried and ironed all the bridesmaid dresses that night and like me wondered what was going to hit us next. We didn't have to wait long. It was the weather. It rained and it snowed. Then I went to the hairdresser. She thought it would be a good idea to tie up my hair in a tight bun. This only succeeded in pulling the corners of my eyes up, making me look slightly Chinese.

Now, you would have thought that the gremlins would

have some sympathy for me by this stage, wouldn't you? No such luck. My dress had a ten foot train that hung from the shoulders. The two tiny bridesmaids should have held this off the wet floor as I walked into the church. However as soon as I started to walk down the aisle one of the little mites saw her mum. She then dropped the train and ran over it, leaving tiny little footprints as she went. She then refused point blank to return to her position. She was going to stop with her mum. The other little girl obviously decided she wasn't going to do the job on her own, and the train was left to drag on the floor. Halfway down the aisle, I felt as if I was being pulled back. Was this some mischievous spirit telling me not to go on? Was it hell!! The dropped train was now soaking up all the dirty snow and water that had been brought in on the feet of my guests. Five feet of pure white silk material now gave a good imitation of an old mop. Once again, I thought, good match for the cake!

Ken and I stood in front of a very severe-looking vicar and waited impatiently for his first words.

'Ladies and gentlemen, I am very sorry the church is so cold, I'm afraid the heating is not working. [Well it wouldn't be, would it?] After the service, please do not throw confetti in the church grounds. If you would care to make a donation to the church restoration fund, you will find a collection box at the door on your way out, thank you.'

The rest of the ceremony held very little magic for me. I was even glad to get it over with, and so were a lot of freezing friends and relatives.

Was that omen number eight or nine? I've lost count, but the comedy continues! The photographer didn't bother to turn up. Ken then informed me at the reception that he had smashed up his car two nights before. He waited patiently, like any loving husband would, for me to recover from this shock. Then he calmly told me that he was singing for the next two nights in Chesterfield, so we would have to have a working honeymoon. What more could a new bride ask for?

The flat that he had promised we would share after the wedding turned out to be a figment of his imagination. So we were homeless. I found a grubby little flat to start our married life in, which must have lasted all of six weeks, for that was when he left me to go to Butlins, and I was certainly not expected to accompany him.

My marriage lasted, on and off, for about three miserable years. We parted amicably; I hated his guts as much as he hated mine. There was a long hard bitter fight for possessions that we either didn't really have, or hadn't totally paid for. At the end of the day, I guess, he was just as glad to be rid of me as I was to be rid of him. The only good thing to come out of my marriage to Ken are my two daughters. Sarah and Isobel. Since Ken's stage image was not enhanced by being 'Daddy', he was more than pleased to leave me to get on with the rearing of our offspring.

See what I mean! If the psychic side of your brain sends you messages, *listen*, for God's sake, listen. For there is nothing more certain than the fact that if you don't, the gremlins will crawl out of the woodwork. Or old wives' tales will be told to you until you go deaf, preferably in both ears. Then you'll be inundated with claptrap, closely followed by superstitious nonsense, and finally suffocated by my all time favourite, coincidence.

6   An Education in Intuition

The psychic side of my brain was by now so totally disillusioned with me that it went on strike, leaving me to stew in my own juices. For two years it stagnated like a temperamental prima donna waiting for an audience worthy enough to appreciate its many and varied abilities. I, meanwhile, was completely oblivious to the fact that, one of my finer senses was now dormant, and continued with my life as if nothing had happened.

During this time, a number of important things happened to me. To start with I gave birth to a beautiful baby girl. She weighed in at eight and a half pounds and had the most fantastic head of auburn hair. The nurses were enchanted and the poor little mite had to suffer three baths a day, purely because every nurse wanted to style her hair. She was absolutely gorgeous; a mother could not have wished for more.

It was whilst I was in hospital, recovering from the birth of Sarah, that my mother brought me *the* magazine that helped me to understand psychic power, psychic people and indeed, myself! It was only an ordinary woman's magazine, one that you could pick up any day, anywhere. But to me it was the start of a new life and a new understanding.

The article was all about fortune-telling with cards and scrying with a crystal ball. (Scrying is an ancient method of looking into the future. The basic idea is that if you concentrate hard as you gaze into the depths of a reflective surface, such as a mirror, pool of water or a crystal ball, all will be revealed to you. Apparently, the great astrologer Nostradamus acquired most of his prophecies by scrying into a brass bowl full of water.) It also included palmistry, graphology and various other methods of predicting the future for those curious and brave enough to look. I was spellbound. I must have read it a dozen times. Then I sent out for more. Nurses went to the library for me and friends rummaged around every bookshop they happened to pass. One of the nurses who was also interested in fortune-telling, went out and brought me a pack of playing cards. Since there was a section on reading cards in the magazine we decided to have a go. We sat there till all hours of the morning, placing the cards exactly as the book directed and attempting to make sense of what they were trying to tell us. All too frequently we had to refer back to the book. It was a great way to pass the time, but it was, oh, so painfully slow!

I soon tired of this laborious process and decided to, shall we say, spice things up a bit. All too soon my activities were attracting half the medical staff that were on night-shift. So when a new nurse visited my bedside I felt it was my duty to liven up what would almost certainly be a long and arduous night for doctors and nurses alike. So I would simply close my eyes and visualize what the mysterious future had in store for them.

It was in these moments, with my eyes closed to the world and my heart eager to please the anticipating client, that I would find the juicy little titbits that made the readings much more interesting and very realistic. Not just for the client, but for me as well. It was these spicy bits that all too often hit home. Every now and again the reaction I got would be pure shock. 'How the hell did you know that?' they would say or, 'Who's been talking to you?'

At this early stage in my learning I wasn't sure whether the nurses were leading me on, or whether indeed I was leading them on. But for a whole week nurse after nurse turned up at my bedside for a reading and a laugh.

Even then, whilst I was still learning to foretell the future, I knew it was going to be essential to keep my readings light-hearted and interesting. This was very important to me. Any prophecy of gloom or doom was neatly tucked to the back of my mind and ignored. I believe this was because, at that time, I would have been unable to cope with the consequences. Not only for the client but for myself, and in truth, my sanity!

I was in hospital for fourteen days, which was fairly normal then. During this period, I spent more time learning about myself and psychic power than I did about the feeding and rearing of a baby. A new baby that very soon was going to depend on me for her every need. As luck would have it, I was a very practical young woman, and if I was unsure about any of the countless facets of child rearing, there was always Mum, who proved to be a wonder-woman. What she didn't know about babies and young children wasn't worth knowing. Then there was the back-up team! Dad and the rest of the family, who could well and truly be relied on to point out my all too many miscellaneous misdemeanours.

I left hospital with a beautiful baby daughter, a new interest in life and a fresh insight into myself. This made me more confident and curious and a lot less confused. Suddenly I knew, I wasn't different or strange, just *psychic*. Now all I had to do was understand exactly what this entailed, and then learn how to harness this truly supreme gift.

Not much happened over the next few years. I moved to Horncastle to be closer to my parents. My ever-roaming husband returned, yet again. I soon became pregnant and was very happy to produce a second child. It didn't seem right to bring Sarah up without the love of brothers or sisters, especially since I had so many happy memories of growing up in what is now considered a large family.

Horncastle was a lovely place to live – more of a charming village than a town, which is its official classification. My parents quickly settled there. I, on the other hand, still desired the city life. So even though I was five months into my second pregnancy, I decided to return to my home town of Nottingham.

It was then that I finally decided to divorce Ken and settled down to a fairly secure life. I didn't have the problems that a lot of one parent families have, because Mum and Dad were never very far away from me if I needed them, for cash or comfort.

The only psychic thing that happened during this time

was not entirely to do with me. Just before the birth of my second daughter, five days to be precise, I went into labour, having frequent and strong contractions, but no pain. This condition continued for the next four days but since there was no pain, I felt there was no reason to panic (they say ignorance is bliss). The fifth day was a Sunday. My brother John phoned me up and asked if I would like to join him and his family for a lunch-time drink. I jumped at the chance to escape from the house. Sarah was briskly washed and dressed and the already prepared dinner was put on hold. Within half an hour, I arrived at the Major Oak. This was a pub that had recently been built conveniently close to my brother's house. I sat with Ivy, my sister-in-law, most of the time whilst John talked to the men. When I told Ivy that I had been having contractions for almost five days she nearly hit the roof and told me not to be so 'bloody stupid' and to 'phone the midwife, immediately'. There was no arguing with her. She wouldn't give me my drink and virtually dragged me to the phone. I got pretty much the same reaction from the midwife, who told me she would be with me in about ten minutes. This proved to be slightly embarrassing, as I had to admit that I was phoning from a public house. She must have thought I was an alcoholic to be having a drink whilst I was actually in labour. I eventually arrived home and found a midwife with the voice and attitude of a sergeant-major waiting on the doorstep for me. She was obviously not amused, and I was annoyed at being caught having what was a very rare drink. I meekly, but begrudgingly, followed her orders. Well, she was bigger than me, even if I was nine months pregnant. As soon as she had examined me, she mumbled something about stupid young women having no more sense than they were born with. She then sent for the doctor, who in turn sent for the ambulance.

I was raced to the hospital, lights flashing, bells ringing. I was stupid enough to ask the driver if we were going to an accident. I hadn't realized the alarms were for me. I don't know who was more relieved – me that there was no emergency, or the driver that I wasn't about to give birth there and then in his ambulance!

Since, like a lot of women, I find the actual process of giving birth uncomfortable, to say the least, I will spare you the gory details. What I must tell you is that this birth was almost completely painless. No gas and air, no drugs and certainly no injections.

Within five minutes of the first doctor seeing me the announcement came. 'You have a lovely baby girl.' That mite was the ugliest thing I had ever seen, so long and thin, her little hands and fingers resembling a curled up spider. She was black and blue with bruises, which the doctor very kindly informed me was my fault, due to the fact that I had lost a lot of the protective water that surrounds a baby during my five days of painless labour. Poor Isobel, what a start to life, only a mum could have loved her then. But when the bruises disappeared and she gained a little weight my ugly little bug turned into the proverbial beautiful butterly.

I phoned Mum and Dad within fifteen minutes of the birth, to let them know we were fit and well. Mum was over the moon, especially since she thought I had another three weeks to go. Now she could stop worrying about me. When I asked her to put Dad on the phone she hesitated, then said he was out with his mates and she couldn't get hold of him. Now Mum is a great woman, but she can't lie to save her life, and I knew something was wrong. Just as I was about to start the Spanish Inquisition, Dad's deep, warm, lilting tones echoed lazily down the line.

'Hayh-up gal, what you bin up to?'

The sound of his voice washed away any doubts that I may have had at that moment. I was so glad to hear his matter-of-fact voice. We talked for a few moments, then as Dad didn't particularly like using the phone, he promised to see me very soon, and said goodbye. This was as good as a sleeping draught for me. Happily I drifted into a long, peaceful, undisturbed slumber.

Weeks later I found out why Mum had hesitated, lied even, when I'd asked her to put Dad on the phone. Apparently Dad had been very ill for five days before the birth of Isobel. He had been suffering with chronic stomach pains. The doctor had sent him to the local hospital for tests. They in turn had attempted to make him stay in overnight because he was in so much pain. But as usual, if Dad could walk, he'd get to his own bed, which is just what he did on this occasion.

Mum had been so very worried, not only about Dad, but also about me, being so close to having the baby. The last thing she wanted was for me to find out that the one man in the world who I worshipped was so ill he should have been in hospital. And so stubborn he would not listen to the quacks, as he used to call them.

So when I phoned to announce Isobel's arrival, Mum decided, for the time being at least, the less I knew the better it was for me. However, just as she was about to put down the phone, Dad had appeared at her side and had taken the phone from her hands. Mum said she was amazed to see him standing at the bar (they were publicans at that time). He was his old self again and more than well enough to wet the baby's head with a very relieved Mum and many of the customers.

To this day I am certain that Dad had indeed had all my labour pains for me. It may sound daft, but there was always an uncanny bond between Isobel and her grandad. He never made more fuss of her than he did the rest of his grandchildren, but there was a quietness between them, an understanding that bridged the span of years. It was almost as if they knew exactly what each other was thinking or even feeling.

Isobel would quietly end up on his knee when he was asleep. He very rarely disturbed, except to protectively put his arm around her. Then with her head resting on his chest and her little arm tucked under his cardigan, they would continue their afternoon nap together in that old armchair.

The saddest thing about this uncanny and lovely relationship between grandad and grandaughter was that Dad died just before Isobel's fifteenth birthday and so I now find Isobel's birthday a mixture of happiness for her, but also of great sadness for me. I miss him so much at this time, I tend to wallow in self-pity. Then I have to walk alone, or hide, so that no one can see me cry. All the time I know Mum must miss him much more than I do, but this is a time when I'm only interested in myself.

They say time is a great healer, but no amount of time is going to make this pain any easier. I just have to learn to live with it, and try to be glad that I had a Dad who lived life to the full and enjoyed teaching us to love and live in a world that has so much to offer. He certainly made sure that we had the happiest and safest childhood possible. The only thing is, I now have one hell of a problem; learning to live without him . . . .

7   Why Tarot?

When I first decided to read cards, I started with a standard pack of fifty-two playing cards. I thoroughly enjoyed using these cards for about six months, and I did learn a lot from them. But every time I opened a book or magazine, I could guarantee that the great tarot cards would reign supreme. There would be about two paragraphs on the use of ordinary cards. Then chapter after chapter on the great and illustrious tarot cards and how that particular author related to them. Then of course, there were always the glorious illustrations of the twenty-two major arcana cards, displayed tantalizingly across the centre page. Oh yes; it was all too easy to change to tarot, even though they were more expensive cards and at times difficult to acquire. It was obvious that, if I was going to be a good reader or indeed a successful reader, then I had to be a tarot card reader. So there I was, with enough literature on tarot to open my own bookshop. One brand new pack of tarot cards and a poor redundant, tattered pack of playing cards. These had served me so well I felt guilty about sending them into early retirement.

For two years I studied each and every card, until I knew the whole pack of seventy-eight back to front and upside down, which for me was no easy task. Then I had to learn where and how to lay the cards and the many possible intricate combinations. I ask you, is it any wonder I was confused? I persevered. I followed the wise ways of one knowledgeable psychic after another and devoured the words of the famous, even brilliant authors, all to no avail. Something was missing. I was still lost and the more I read the less I understood. The less I understood, the more curious and frustrated I became.

I had worked and worked hard. I desperately needed some sort of reward. It was as if someone had said to me, 'Go on Kris, climb that mountain, there's a big pot of gold waiting for you at the top. It's all yours, it's got your name on it, no one else can claim it.' So I climbed, and I worked hard, but on reaching the top, nothing! No understanding, no reward, no goal and certainly no gold. Just the tantalizing glints of gold from the next mountain, so far away.

Obviously I felt like giving up. The frustration was unbelievable. Then one night, after two years of studying tarot, but not necessarily understanding how tarot worked with psychic vision, I had it all explained to me by a man, an extraordinary man, with no name. He came to me in a dream and refused to leave me until I understood all that he had to say, which was all that I needed to know.

I must have slept soundly the first night he visited me; I usually do. Only this time as I slipped from reality into the realms of dream world, I found myself looking across a vast and beautiful desert. I could actually feel the sand beneath my feet. My shoulders and cheeks tingled in the warm sunshine. I was totally alone. The movement of the dry sand fascinated me, leaving no room for fear of this strange exquisite vision. Whilst I sat on the warm sand, the analytical side of my brain attempted to find a gear it could work in. Somehow I knew I was safe, so why shouldn't I take the opportunity and bask in the balmy heat of the sun and sand? After all, how long can a dream last, especially one this good?

The sand had the texture of fine clean salt; I'd never seen sand this clean. It sparkled as I allowed it to run slowly and silently through my fingers and down my legs. My eyes lazily scanned the horizon, not that I was looking for anything or indeed anyone. No, I was simply absorbing the bewitching, unreal view. Mile upon panoramic mile of burnished sand lay before me. This was a vision that had to be savoured. I wanted to etch it into my brain, well aware that this may have been my first and last visit to this strange and powerful land.

A gentle warm wind blew around me as I drank in the

view. Then somewhere in that breeze I heard someone whisper my name.

'Kris, Kris.'

The sound of my name startled me. Suddenly I was wide awake and staring at the ceiling. My mind raced with the possibilities. Was it a vision, had someone been trying to contact me? If so, why me? If it was indeed just a dream, why was it so clear, different and yet so real? I reluctantly returned to sleep, knowing that this was a dream I would remember for a long time to come. What I did not know was that I would return to that very same desert in the near future.

Three uneventful nights passed. I was beginning to think that it was just an unusual dream after all and began to put the whole thing to the back of my mind. On the fourth night as I blissfully slept I heard the voice whispering again.

'Kris, Kris, come, you know you're safe with me.'

Inexplicably, my mind and body relaxed, and then I drifted deeper and deeper into a sleep that allowed me once again to visit, without fear, the unknown!

The desert appeared before me – warm, clean and bright, cordially inviting me to enjoy the pleasures that it held. I sat once again on the clean dry sand and looked around me. This time, a figure clothed from head to toe in a white robe stood about thirty feet in front of me. A brown weathered face smiled at me from beneath the hood. There was something familiar about him. I couldn't place it then and I certainly can't now, but his very presence put my every sense at ease. He held out his hand, beckoning me to follow him. I had every intention of doing precisely that when suddenly he disappeared. I was slowly being drawn back to reality and found myself as you would expect; in bed, wide awake and wondering!

The next night I knew I was going to see my mystery man. His very aura surrounded me, even before I retired to my bed. So it came as no surprise when my body and mind, released from the shackles of reality, settled me gently close to him, on the sands of the desert. We were so close this time that we almost touched as we now viewed the landscape. Like old friends, we spent a few quiet moments together, our hearts and minds entwined and content, away from the rigours of time.

The view was breathtaking, its simplicity unbelievably beautiful. Ripples and mounds of sand that for all the world looked as if they had been created by some great sculptor out of glowing gold. Shadows caressed the sand like an ever-moving blanket, continually changing the scene, revealing a new image that was just as serene as the last. I could have sat there forever, but his oh, so gentle, strong voice invaded my thoughts.

'Some men fear the view you seem to enjoy Kris. Others see it as a challenge and want to cross it, build on it, or preserve it. Many love, hate, or don't even care about it.' He paused, taking up a handful of sand, then allowed it to fall slowly to the ground. 'There are as many views of this desert Kris, as there are grains of sand in my hand. None of them are right or wrong, only different. No two people will have quite the same view or feelings. You have to use your own eyes to see Kris, your own heart to feel. No one can teach you to love or listen, to feel or see. No one can interpret your psychic visions.'

We sat still and quiet, whilst I digested his words. I didn't need him to explain further. What I did need now was an opportunity to sort out my thoughts. There was so much to do. I had got to be myself and not a replica of any famous author or psychic, dead or alive. It was time for a new beginning. It was time for me, Kris Sky, psychic, to climb the right mountain.

I turned to look into his deep brown eyes. He smiled at me, then took both of my hands in his, gently pulling me to my feet.

'I'll always be there if you need me Kris, but now I must go. There are many, like you, who need my guidance so that they in turn may help others. Now you can get on with your life, free from the bonds of confusion. It's no longer necessary for you to conform to other people's standards, it's time for you to trust your own.'

His hands slipped from mine, then he turned to walk slowly across the desert. As I lost sight of him, I felt myself being drawn back, unwillingly, to reality. All too soon I was staring at that familiar ceiling above my head, I rose from my bed and headed for the kitchen. I needed a coffee, but more important, I had to start making plans. There was a lot to do, and I intended to do it well, my way.

Over the next few weeks I worked like a devil possessed. I totally dismissed all that I had previously learned and casually ignored the mountains of written literature that I had amassed over the years. I was going to create my own method of reading the cards, one that would relate to today's people and today's problems. So, out went the Celtic cross and the tree of life, along with the mystic star, the fan and the temple of fortune.

I had to decide exactly what was liable to be important to any future customer who desired a reading. I started with what would be crucial for me, if I were the client. What sort of useful information would I require from a psychic or fortune-teller? I expected the list to be endless, but it wasn't – it was surprisingly short.

Health and wealth were the first two categories I thought were essential. Closely followed by love, life, and ambition. I felt it would also be useful to analyse a client's character, home life, and work life; past, present and future. Then, since life has a nasty habit of pulling the rug from under one's feet just when one least expects it, it would also be necessary to produce a whole section that dealt with life's little surprises.

My list completed, I now had to fathom out how I was going to lay the cards in order to make the most of them. The spread was kept simple, though I did try to adhere to some of the ancient rules. However, the age-old custom of the cards having an alternative meaning if they appeared upside down was just too much for me, so that had to go. Each and every one of the cards now had a fresh, new and true meaning for me. So it seemed ridiculous that they should mean the opposite, just because they were inverted.

Soon I was ready to try out my own new method of reading cards and there was no shortage of friends for me to practice on. These friends also provided me with lots of new blood. Stranger after stranger was dragged in by my faithful mates so that I could practice on them and, I can assure you, they were often just as pleased and astonished as I was. Within two years I felt I was ready for anything the world had to throw at me, which was just as well, because I wasn't quite prepared for Sue Burrows. My mystery man in the dreams may have helped me to develop my gift, but Sue was the one who convinced me it was a saleable asset!

8   Amateur or Professional?

The years fled by while I read hands, tea-leaves, sands and stones. Anything to amuse my friends, but most of all I read tarot cards. Slowly but surely I was beginning to understand how they worked with my type of clairvoyant vision. The psychic side of my brain that had previously been on strike was now working overtime.

My children were growing up, and I had chosen my second husband. To start with the marriage was a little rocky, mainly because over the years I had become a little bombastic. I'd been on my own for so long I'd forgotten how to depend on any man, other than my father. Despite this, John and I were able to solve most of our problems and eventually we were as close as any couple could be.

John had served nine years as a royal marine and was used to working hard. Civvy Street only offered him two choices: the dole or the mines. He wasn't the type to be on the dole, so he decided to work at the local pit. All my old fears returned. I hated the thought of him going down that bloody hole, but he wouldn't listen. All he would say was, 'If that's where the money is that's where I'm going.' I had little or no say in it. John was determined to provide as well as he could for his ready-made family and the new baby I was expecting.

John was daft about kids. If it had been left to him we would have had a dozen. However, as soon as I had successfully produced a son and a daughter, I managed to persuade him that I was getting a bit long in the tooth to carry children.

All the time that John was working down the pit, my reputation for reading cards was growing. Not only that, people were now coming from near and far to see me.

John did not approve of my interest in the occult and one night his disapproval caused an almighty argument.

We had gone to the local club for a drink, which we usually did at the weekend. On arrival I was kidnapped to read the cards in a quiet room at the top of the club. This happened all too often, but this night I was in that room from eight o'clock till eleven and the only drink I'd had was the first one! John was furious; enough was enough. Either I stopped reading cards or he would stop bringing me out. He was fed up of taking me out, only to see me disappear within moments to read cards. John was adamant. My card reading days were over! My marriage to John was, and still is, much more important to me than proving my psychic ability or amusing my friends. So I reluctantly settled down to the odious duty of obeying the male chauvinist pig. Not an easy task for someone like me who finds any sort of barrier or rule an irresistible challenge.

They say it's an ill wind that blows no good. This was very true for me. John had been suffering stomach pains for a number of years. When they finally decided to operate, they discovered he had stomach ulcers. The first operation was far from successful, which meant poor John had to return to hospital a year later, for even more treatment under the surgeon's knife.

Obviously he was out of work for some time. Money was getting short, when a friend of mine, Sue Burrows, said 'Why don't you read the cards Kris, go professional? You're more than good enough.' Now reading cards for fun or to test my ability was one thing. Reading for money was quite a different cup of tea. I wasn't at all sure if I was ready to go professional, and anyway, in the past I had never charged. All I received was the proverbial cross your palm with silver act. I didn't know if I had the guts to charge, and more important, what would John say?

The germ of an idea that Sue had planted began to grow in my brain like a weed in a garden. The more I ignored it, the faster it grew. I had to know more. Silly little questions kept cropping up, like how much would I charge and how in hell's name do I get started? Then I had to know how a true professional performed. Believe it or not, I had never seen a clairvoyant or fortune-teller in my life. This problem was soon overcome. Sue quickly made arrangements for four of us to visit a woman who lived about six miles away. I was about to see my first clairvoyant.

Two days later, four anxious and slightly sceptic women, namely us, arrived at an ordinary little house on what looked to be a nice council estate. Someone rang the bell and a young blonde woman answered the door and invited us in. It turned out that she was the clairvoyant, much to my disappointment. Somehow I expected her to be old and definitely dark. Lesson number one, I thought!

We were led into the lounge, then she took Sue through to a back room. The front doorbell rang continuously and kids were running in and out of the house making one hell of a noise. I don't know what I worried about most, the clairvoyant not being able to concentrate, or her kids wrecking the house. To say nothing of paying £3.50 that I could ill afford at that time. I made up my mind there and then, if she was no good, I certainly wasn't going to pay her. After about forty minutes Sue stuck her head round the door and told the next one, her sister, to go in. Once the door was shut, we all got our heads together to discuss Sue's reading.

Sue was suitably impressed with the session. She was quite delighted when the woman told her she had a big black and white dog. I did wonder, cynically maybe, if the small amount of dog hairs on Sue's black corduroy dress could have been a dead giveaway. Sue went on to say that the clairvoyant had been able to pick up quite a few facts that related to her past and also predicted that she would have a daughter in the future. This was just what Sue wanted and as it happens proved to be quite true. Our discussion was cut short; the clairvoyant was now ready to see me.

I hesitated warily in the doorway of what turned out to be the kitchen. She saw my apprehension, then quickly bade me to sit down in front of her. Somehow a reading conducted alongside the day's pots was not quite what I was expecting. Lesson number two now registered securely at the back of my brain. She took hold of both my hands and told me to close my eyes. Then she closed hers.

You'll have guessed at this stage in the game, that I was peeping! She started to speak, her voice soft and slow.

'You have a grandfather in the spirit world,' she said. It took me a few seconds to realize she was actually speaking to me. As soon as my mouth and brain were in the same gear, I replied.

'Yes, I suppose I do.'

So she carried on. 'He was very old when he passed on. Old and tired. He's now showing me his gold fob watch and he's wearing a flat cap. He wants you to know that he still loves you, but he was glad to go, he was in so much pain.'

She went quiet, which gave me the opportunity to ask, 'Are you sure it's my grandad?'

'Yes dear,' she said, 'if it's not on your mother's side, then it must be on your father's.'

I felt this was a good time to be honest, since both my grandads had been fairly young when they passed on and their deaths unexpected. Neither of them fitted her description, especially since Mum's dad was a red-head and very agile, right up to the end. He died when I was about four, so I have very little memory of him. Then there was a story in our family that my grandad on my father's side had given Dad instructions to 'drown the first child' my mum was already expecting, 'if it was a girl' but 'give it five bob if it was a lad'. So it was lucky that my brother entered the world a good four years before I did. I still think grandad and I would have got on, despite his instructions.

The clairvoyant listened to my descriptions of my two grandads, then said sharply, 'It must be one of your great-grandads then.'

Now, since I have never seen a great-grandad, I was in no position to argue, so she went on with the reading.

'You will have a child in three years that will bring you great joy.'

I assured her that if I did I would be suing the hospital, because I'd been sterilized after giving birth to my fourth child.

'Ah yes,' she said, 'I can see them now, what lovely children.'

Now this bit was true, but it had become pretty obvious that the reading was not going at all well. I was not about to become her favourite customer so it was time to change tactics. She wriggled in her chair as she shuffled a few tarot cards. A small mixture of about twenty major and minor arcana cards were placed ceremoniously on the table. My expectations were high. I had great faith in the tarot. All her misdemeanours were instantly dismissed. I listened intently.

'You will have great wealth late in life. One of your children will become a nurse, and your husband will never leave you. £3.50 please.'

I was so taken aback by her attitude that I meekly paid up. The one thing this reading did teach me was that I couldn't possibly be worse!

I went on to see more clairvoyants, along with a sprinkling of mediums, tea-leaf readers, crystal ball scryers and astrologers. To say the least I was not impressed. I needed someone, anyone, to prove to me that it was possible to see into the future. I had to know that I was not alone, and more important, that I was not like the readers that I'd met, who were only after easy money.

These so-called professionals set my mind in a turmoil. I had to ask myself question after question. Did I expect too much? Were my friends too easily pleased? Or did they hear only what they wanted to? Maybe all psychics are con merchants? Maybe they start out with good intentions, but lose interest in all but the money as time goes by. Perhaps they, and indeed I, have delusions of grandeur. Is there a possibility that we are all plain crazy? I had to do an awful lot of soul-searching to find the answers to all these questions and many more, before I could set up as a professional clairvoyant. If I was going to enter this weird and wonderful profession, I was going in with my eyes wide open and a damn good moral code of conduct.

Setting up business had its fair share of practical problems. To start with, I required a phone and a place to work from that had to be quiet. I needed a good name that would be easy to recognize and remember, so I slightly altered my own. Then business cards had to be designed and printed. If I was going to start work, I was going to be professional.

Sue solved most of my problems. She became my manager and chauffeur, and allowed me to work from her home. She even put my first advert in the local newspaper and decided that I should charge, to start with, that memorable figure, £3.50. Now all Sue had to do was persuade both John and myself that I could and would succeed. I expected John to go mental when I told him of my intentions to set up as a clairvoyant, but this was one time when he certainly surprised me. He listened to what I'd got to say, asked a few questions, then, like some long-suffering male, who's bored to death with female prattlings said, 'Well, if that's what you want to do, and the kids don't suffer, go ahead, but don't go visiting any strange houses unless Sue is with you.'

Obviously John thought this was just a passing phase I was going through. I'm sure he was under the impression that if he treated the idea with the contempt he thought it deserved, it would soon go away.

Within twenty-four hours of that advert being placed. I was in business. Sue was as nervous as I was when I went out to my first engagement, but she made me go and I don't think I ever looked back. The work rolled in, I loved meeting people and I thoroughly enjoyed reading for them. It was at this early stage that I made these solemn promises: To be true to myself and never to make up stories just to please the client. To try not to get greedy for the money or the glory. And finally, never to put my work before my family. With these promises etched deeply in my brain, I continued to work with Sue for the best part of a year.

My husband John (despite his initial disapproval), was always there to encourage me if I was low, or put me back in my place if I started to get airs and graces! So my feet were kept safely on the ground, which was just as well because the more readings I did the more confident I became. Then, just as I was beginning to think I was the greatest thing since sliced bread, the rug was pulled out from under my feet. My world and my confidence was shattered; suddenly I was playing with the unknown.

9   The Day I Spoke Russian

The day started much the same as any other. I dressed and fed the kids, then did most of the cleaning. Sue phoned to tell me that I would be working from five o'clock onwards at her house, and to make sure that I had a baby-sitter for the night. I assured Sue that John would be home in time to look after the children so there was no problem. I actually arrived at Sue's about fifteen minutes early. This gave me the chance to catch up with all the gossip over a nice cup of coffee. Just before my clients arrived, Sue picked up her son and headed off to her mother's for a few hours, giving me the freedom and more importantly, the quietness of her home.

My client arrived with a friend in tow. No one had to be clairvoyant to see that the woman I was about to read for was very ill. She was not so old, only about fifty, but her body was tired and her blue eyes were deep and sad. The depression that surrounded her enveloped me. I felt I had shared all her pain and sadness. Then she smiled and the moment was gone.

She introduced herself and her friend, then apologized for being so slow on her feet. She was tall, about five feet ten inches, but stooped. If she had been able to stand up straight, I thought that she could have been a ballet dancer in her younger days. Her illness may have bent and weakened her body, but her face still held pride and it was easy to see she had once been very attractive.

We left her friend in the front room of the house and went through to the quieter middle room where I did all my readings.

She sat down opposite me, then looked me straight in the eyes and said, 'Don't be afraid to tell me all you see, because I'm not afraid.'

My answer was very slow and deliberate. Without further hesitation I said, 'You're dying. You have very little time left.'

'I know,' she said, 'now please go on.'

There were no tears, no shock, very little reaction at all from her, except for a slightly bemused look on her face. She knew that I had only just realized the inevitability of what I'd said, and that at that moment, I was the one having difficulty coping with such a drastic statement. Commonsense was beginning to take over and my mind stopped spinning enough to allow me to speak.

'How on earth can I read your cards when you have so little time left? I don't want to waste your money.'

'My dear,' she said slowly, 'I'm not worried about money, or you reading the cards. I'm here because something or someone has drawn me to you. For over a week now, a voice in my dreams has been calling your name, over and over again. I have been told to come to you, some invisible force has driven me to you and only you. I don't know who or why, but there has to be a reason so I'm here.'

Slightly bewildered, I gave her the cards to shuffle. This was just a delaying tactic which gave me the opportunity to reorganize my thoughts. I didn't know how I was going to help her. I had never been so close to a person who knew they were about to die. What was I going to say or do that could possibly help her? The cards were shuffled and cut so I began to deal them, much the same way as I would do for any of my clients. I started with her personality and past life. I was right! She had done ballet as a child, but only for her own enjoyment and not attaining any professional standard. Her early life was full of misery. Many of her family had passed on early and even the fiancé who had captured her heart had died in a car crash, leaving her lost and alone for what must have seemed an eternity.

Time passed. Eventually she made a new, but somewhat empty, lonely life for herself. Travelling the world and making friends but never finding anyone to quite fill the gap in her heart. Now she had cancer and was fast coming to the end of her life. There was no miracle cure and she knew, no hope.

The cards became blurred. My head began to feel tight, as if someone were squeezing my head between their large strong hands. My mouth became dry, I started to mumble. Strange words rolled with some difficulty off my tongue, I felt as if I were losing control of my body and my mind! The only connection I had with myself and what I knew to be my world was the table that I now gripped on to until my hands had gone white. That large circular dark glass table acted as an anchor for me. An anchor that kept me safely attached to a world that I dearly loved and was in no hurry to leave. I went hot, cold and sticky all in a matter of seconds. Sweat began to trickle down my face. Someone or something had now taken over my very thoughts and I didn't even know what I was saying. The darkness began to swirl around me as tears, hot and stinging, filled my eyes, but I was not about to let go of that table.

'Go on, Go on!' my client was pleading with me, begging me to continue. Or was she pleading with the spirit that now occupied my body?

'Please go on, I do understand, I do understand.' Her pleading encouraged me to carry on, even though I was scared stiff. Her long delicate hands grasped mine and suddenly they had a new-found power. Whether she was taking my strength or I hers is debatable. Perhaps the bond in itself drew on an unknown force. I really didn't know, but it was there, and it was very real! I had little choice but to submit to this strange, powerful entity. The gibberish words spilled from my mouth with ease for what seemed ages but must have only been a few moments. Then, slowly as if waking from a deep sleep, my head started to clear. My hands felt as if they had been in a vice; every inch of me was icy cold.

I looked at my client, not knowing what to expect. There she sat, calm and glowing, staring just above my head. Her eyes were full of tears but she was smiling.

'I'm sorry,' I said, still confused, not knowing what had really happened. I was under the impression that I had had a brainstorm and that this woman must have thought

I was mad. I was certainly beginning to wonder. Her eyes met mine, then she spoke.

'Now I know why I had to see you. Now I know why your name has been whispered to me so often whilst I have slept.' She paused, obviously tired. 'For a brief moment you were my mother! A mother who I loved dearly.' She continued with her story. 'Momma died in a concentration camp whilst I was a little girl. We are Russian you know. You were speaking Russian, just like Momma. You even used her pet name for me, which was "little dove". I now know that there is life after death. I can't begin to thank you enough.'

It was at this stage that I actually found the courage to let go of the table. I stood up, wanting to stretch my cold, almost numb legs. My client wiped the tears from her eyes, and asked me to fetch her friend from the front room. Arm in arm they walked slowly and quietly to the front door that I had opened for them. Then taking my hand once more she said, 'Thank you, Kris, you have been a great help to me, I hope your God is good to you.' With that they got into the waiting car and waved goodbye.

I closed the door and went through to the middle room. I was so cold I went to put on the gas fire, but found it was already on. I should have been warm, not cold. Then I went to get a comb out of my bag. My long, dark, unruly hair needs combing often. I went to the mirror and there, looking back at me was the dirtiest face I had seen in my life. Black dirty rivers running from my eyes, down my cheeks and onto my neck. I was amazed, then worried. What had my client thought of me? It looked as if I had put on loads of dark make-up and it had run. This was the only logical answer. However, I never wear make-up in the day and I always wash any off, if I wear it at night, ritualistically before I go to bed. I almost ran to Sue's kitchen sink to wash off the dark sticky greyish dirt, using washing-up liquid in my haste to get rid of it. Much, much later when I recalled the story to a medium, he nearly cried, saying I had almost certainly washed away *ectoplasm*.

Susan had a party that night, but I was too tired to go. When I saw Sue the next day she told me that they nearly had to fetch me. Apparently Jane, one of the guests, had sat in the same chair that I had sat in the previous afternoon. Suddenly Jane felt terribly cold and frightened. She ran from the room saying something was wrong but couldn't explain what she'd felt. It took them ages to calm her down in the kitchen and some of the guests thought she was just being hysterical. But I knew what had happened. As soon as Sue told me, I knew!

I had not told Sue or anyone what had transpired in the middle room that afternoon. To start with, I didn't think for one minute anyone would believe me. Then, I must admit, I was a little worried about how Sue and her family would have reacted if I had told them. I can't imagine it's a nice thing to know that spirits have been seen and heard in your own home. It could give some people, even brave people, very restless nights.

Jane certainly didn't know about my Russian visitor. The psychic side of her brain must have made her aware that there had been some sort of presence in that room but no one else felt it. Within twenty-four hours, the incident was forgotten by all except me. I worried all night, wondering if I had left a spirit in limbo.

First thing the next morning I phoned Sue to tell her I had a client that day and would need her middle room to do a reading. Sue quickly told me to help myself. She was going out for the day so there was no problem. Two hours later I arrived at the house and let myself in.

Nervously I sat in the same position, on the same chair as I had two days previous. I spent a full hour patiently waiting to see if I could feel anything at all, silently praying to my own God, that if I had done anything wrong, please could I put things right again. Now it's debatable as to how brave I was going to be. Or what I was going to do if a spirit did turn up, saying something like, 'OK lass, now you have got me here what do you intend to do about it?'

Your guess is as good as mine, but I have this sneaky feeling I may have run a mile.

However, the atmosphere around me was nice and peaceful. Then I had this great feeling that what I had done two days before, or more to the point, what had been done to me, was right, very right. I had helped someone and it felt good! There was no lost spirit drifting about Sue's house. All that was there now was a warm, happy, and peaceful home, much to my relief.

My client did die about four weeks later. Her friend phoned to tell me that even she felt the quality of her friend's life had greatly improved in those last few weeks. The woman herself sent her thanks again and said she hoped to see me again on the other side. But not too soon, as I still had many frightened people to help.

10   Working From Home

This little episode in my career made me realize that I would have to work from home or acquire an office. Then I wouldn't be leaving any of my work problems, or rebellious spirits, in someone else's house. So reluctantly I started to work from my own home. This proved to be much more successful that I had anticipated. I found that I could clean the house, feed the children, or even walk the dog if I so desired, between appointments. My husband and daughters became excellent receptionists, taking all my bookings and only rarely booking me in two places at the same time, invariably many miles apart.

I worried for some time that my chosen career would affect my children and give them strange ideas. But they all appear to have grown up to be quite normal; at least I think so. We've had a few laughs though, like the time when my youngest daughter Christine dragged me up to school to see a painting that she'd done of me. I dutifully trundled around the classroom admiring all that was presented to me, then came face to face with a large hanging mobile of a witch. Christine delighted in telling me that this was indeed her picture of me. She was so proud of it and I had to agree, not only was it very artistic, but much to her teacher's amusement, there was a smattering of likeness. I felt it was necessary to explain to the teacher that I had not led my artistic offspring to believe that I was a witch. This made the teacher laugh and then she assured me that, if I didn't believe half that Christine told me about school, she wouldn't believe half that Christine told her about home. Nevertheless, I told my husband that very night, in no uncertain terms, that he had got to stop calling me 'Winnie the Witch'. I would like to say that he has seen the error of his ways, but all he did was snigger, then ask me sarcastically where I'd left my broomstick.

Another memorable occasion happened when I acquired my first crystal ball. I had placed it in the middle of my reading table, then gone to the kitchen to prepare the dinner. Christine shot in from school, then ran straight upstairs to change into her jeans. She must have spotted the crystal as she passed the reading room door. Screaming with delight, she informed me that there was a crystal ball in my room. I told her that I knew, because I'd put it there. Then came the inevitable.

'Does it work Mum? Can I have a go?'

Well, what could I say except, 'Go on then, but be careful not to drop it.'

Christine was gone for ages, only returning when called for her dinner. She looked a bit down in the mouth, so I asked her what the matter was.

'I can't find the switch,' she said.

'What switch love?' I asked. I suppose I should have known what was coming next. Sometimes mothers do ask the daftest questions when their brains are on hold.

'The switch for the crystal ball. I want to look at the pictures.' John nearly choked on his dinner, which only succeeded in causing even more disruption. All the children, including Christine, found the vision of Dad, laughing, choking and trying to leave the table all at the same time highly amusing. It was a good ten minutes later that John managed to regain some sort of composure. Then the family returned to what was by now a very cold dinner.

A little later on in the day, I tried to explain to Christine, in the very simplest terms, how the crystal was supposed to work. As soon as she found out that there weren't going to be any pretty pictures, she lost all interest, saying that she would rather watch TV. For once I agreed with her.

My children are aware that I am also interested in ghosts, as I have been known to go out on the occasional all night vigil. So they tend to think that ghosts, spooks and things that go bump in the night are a little tame. After all, if Mum's not scared of them, then there can't be much to be scared of, can there?

I once heard some older children trying to frighten my four-year-old son with a really good, spine-chilling, bloodcurdling ghost story. He listened intently whilst they went through every morbid detail. Then quite nonchalantly he piped up with, 'You can bring your ghost to my mum, she loves busting them!', much to the disgust of the by now red-faced story teller.

My children, far from being afraid of my unusual work, actually approve of what I do. They used to think it was great. Mum being a clairvoyant. Well, it is a bit different isn't it? It certainly holds more magic than most everyday jobs, although the novelty of that has now worn off. I believe all children adapt easily to any situation as long as they have full stomachs and are surrounded by love. Mine certainly are!

Enough is enough. You now know all you need to know about my family, my upbringing, and my somewhat lackadaisical ability to raise my own children. I have provided you with as much information as I can, on how my psychic power evolved and affected not only my life, but the life of others around me. It is vital you understand that psychic ability has little to do with a sad, lonely or traumatic upbringing. In fact for me, without the security of a good life, the recognition and development of my psychic ability would have been impossible.

Psychic power dwells within all of us and I'm in no doubt that some sort of emotional trauma can trigger off psychic ability. That same power, without the security of love and the understanding that comes with time, can become twisted and corrupt, often rendering a person mentally unbalanced, or even psychotic.

Remember this and then with a little luck, you too will be able to develop a psychic skill that will not only amaze you, but prove to be a most efficient and useful gift. With this in mind let's press on, for I am certain that you are now curious as to the how, why and when I use my clairvoyant ability professionally.

11   How I See

People tend to confuse clairvoyance with the many other psychic talents that are now available. I am often asked for a love potion or a lucky charm. Then there are others who seek me out because they wish to speak to a loved one who has passed on. Some, more sadly, hope that I have the ability to heal. I would love to be able to help them all, but alas, this is not possible. I do try. Over the years I have become very interested in many of these subjects, but I find that clairvoyance is where my particular skill thrives with an uncanny amount of accuracy.

My job is to look into the future and warn the client of any forthcoming disasters. Then they can prepare themselves or soften the blow. Some pitfalls may be avoided altogether. There is little point in looking forward if you can't make a few small minor alterations. Some people are under the impression that their every step is mapped out for them, and that they can do little or nothing to change their destiny. I do not believe this is so.

Destiny is a little like the M1 with its many junctions, and there's nothing more certain than the fact that there's a beginning and an end, even if someone does keep extending it. It's exactly the same with life. We are born at the start of the road, then have the austere, yet inspiring task of travelling down it, reaching junction after junction, until we reach the inevitable … death.

However, the road is often long, giving us many opportunities to travel in the fast or slow lanes. Then there is the luxury class for those who have a Rolls Royce type of existence and, as usual, an economy class. The only difference is that this time, money will not pay for that first class ticket. Only happiness, a good heart and the ability to love, forgive and forget, permits you to travel in style on the easy road.

Clairvoyance gives you the opportunity to take a good long look at that road. It's a little like travelling in one of those large trucks that are so high off the road. Those drivers can see for miles more down the road than the average driver of the little Mini-type car. All that this driver can usually see is the back of the motor in front of him. A person with a clear view of the road has the time to make any relevant manoeuvre safely, in order to travel at the correct speed at the right time in their life. This may be a faster or slower speed or maybe even a stop. Sometimes, if the road ahead is blocked, they may choose to travel a different, prettier road altogether in order to reach their junction in life, thus making their road or life much better. So you see, all that clairvoyance does is give you the chance to drive a truck with a good clear view of the road ahead instead of your usual motor. This way you will still reach your destiny, points, or junctions in life, but with a little luck, a happier, better, less fraught and more successful person!

Over the years I've been able to help many people drive that truck. Together we have been able to view the road ahead and then, with a little foresight, plan a more suitable route. I sincerely hope that this will be the case with you and that this book will help you to help yourself. For I now intend to help you not only find the clairvoyant side of your brain but get the damn thing to work in your favour. I fear that this is a rather stupid thing to do as I may be putting myself out of a job, but then again I could do with a break! So if you do feel that you are a budding clairvoyant, go out and buy youself a pack of tarot cards. For in the next few pages I intend to reveal many of my own secret psychic methods of reading the tarot cards. I am also determined to destroy many of the myths that prevent true psychic ability from obtaining its proper place in society and science. Psychic power exists and someday soon, society and science will accepts it's existence.

12   Tuning in to Tarot

Tarot cards are not evil and owning a set will certainly not bring you bad luck or even good luck. You won't catch some awful disease handling them and the spirits won't haunt you till your hair goes white or you go stark raving mad. These attractive, intriguing, pieces of card have no power of their own. No! They really don't, I can assure you of that. They are just pretty pictures on stiff card and as such, as harmless as the reproduction Constable of *The Hay Wain* hanging on your lounge or hall wall.

As for intricate pictures on these cards, the set I favour is the usual 'IJJ Swiss Tarot' pack, designed hundreds of years ago. There are many mysterious stories that go with the tarot cards and their original designer. Yet no one has really been able to pin-point their intuitive and obviously psychic creator. Since, as you may well know by now, I am not into research, I will leave you to discover and believe in any legendary epical version that pleases you most. I do not intend to lecture you on the subject of the origins of tarot. I am going to teach you how to use tarot, along with your own hidden psychic power.

First of all let's remember what Psy, my friend from the desert told me, because that one sentence from him contained more useful information than any book ever written on psychic power. He said, 'You have to use your own eyes to see Kris, your own heart to feel. No one can teach you to love or listen, to feel or see. No one can interpret your own psychic visions.'

With this in mind we can now go forward. Free from all the rules and rituals of reading tarot you too can realize your full psychic potential. And I hope, with my guidance, learn how to harness psychic senses with a little commonsense.

I am now going to explain to you how the tarot pack works for me. Remember though, how I feel about a card doesn't necessarily mean that you will feel the same way. Treat each and every card the same way that you would a blind date, or a new lover. Enjoy the excitement and the waiting of the initial introduction. Then decide whether you like the outside appearance of this character or card. Now, you wouldn't toss a blind date to one side just because he or she doesn't come up to your expectations visually. At least I hope you wouldn't, as callous people aren't usually sensitive enough to be psychic. So don't throw the card to one side yet. For now you have to go one stage further and look deeper into the card to discover the finer qualities that remain hidden deep within it as it does with some people. Now you are going to look for the all important personality, heart, and even soul of the card. Then be careful. For just as you become secure in your knowledge and believe that you understand all that there is within that card, a fresh, controversial, and sometimes depressing or enlightening aspect often comes to the forefront. Just like a lover. Something that you had previously been unaware of becomes alarmingly apparent. Like finding that a lover has an ex-wife, or, even worse, still has a wife. On the other hand, if you're lucky (some hope), you could discover that he or she has hidden talents or is a millionaire. But you still have that same love for that same man or woman because he or she hasn't essentially changed. The basic qualities that you originally fell for remain, but now this new insight will force you to reassess your partner. What was once a simple and loving relationship may become complicated, tainted with the pain of jealousy, anger and fear of losing something that possibly wasn't there in the first place. Except in our own hearts or minds.

The tarot cards are truly just like lovers. As you take up each card, you and only you will have to decide whether it makes you feel good or bad, happy or sad, angry or frustrated. There's no point in just reading the cards. Anyone can do that in the same manner that one reads a newspaper or washing instructions off the back of a packet of soap powder. If you really want to experience a psychic tarot card reading you are going to have to get into the cards and use all your senses. You are going to have to look at them and listen to them, smell and feel them. With a little time and patience you will become aware of all the emotions that tarot can and often will bring to the surface. Only when you begin to experience feelings whilst looking into the cards will you truly be using your own psychic power.

If you are going to read tarot it's fairly obvious that you will first need a pack of tarot cards. Then you will require a book in which you can write about your experiences. This book should be kept solely for this purpose. Keep one page for each card and how you have related to it. Don't be too surprised when you discover that your feelings and written statements vary from day to day. To start with you may find there is little to write about, but you must set down your first feelings no matter how simple or how few. As you experiment you should find that a card will continue to produce the same feelings or very similar feelings within you. It's a bit like words, for example, love. This word is used in many areas of our life, but it very rarely means the same thing. We love our parents. We love our children. We love our home, work and food. Finally, with a little luck, we love our spouses. The word itself can be used to interpret many similar feelings, but in truth they can, and frequently are, worlds apart. This is also true of the cards, so be prepared for one lonely card arousing a multitude of feelings. Which is why you will find it necessary to record your thoughts and feelings on paper.

I cannot and will not try to get you to conform to standards that I have created for myself. However, I do feel that the practice of reading inverted cards and giving them a reversed meaning is both time-consuming and senseless. Surely no one in their right mind would have gone to so much trouble creating miniature masterpieces only to turn them upside down. It would be a bit like hanging the *Mona Lisa* upside down in the Louvre – that's how I feel about it anyway. I will now tell you how I feel mentally and physically during a psychic consultation using tarot. I only reveal these very private thoughts and feelings because this will enable you to understand and come to terms with your own psychic experiences. The fact that the cards themselves do appear to change and blend with psychic vision may seen strange, but you will find that this is so. I'm certainly not about to reveal to you all my trade secrets (there's enough competition about nowadays), but what you do learn by reading this book will put you on the right road to learning more about your own psychic ability. Believe me, you do not have to be the seventh son of a seventh son or have gypsy blood coursing through your veins. Nor do you have to have an ancestry that's riddled with mediums, voodoo or witchcraft. Everyone, but everyone, possesses a certain amount of psychic ability. Some choose to ignore it, whilst others attempt to train and enhance the natural psychic gift that they have. As with all gifts, some people are endowed with more talent than others. Lack of superior ability is no reason to totally dismiss the gift as useless. After all, very few of us have a dulcet euphonious singing voice, but that doesn't stop us enjoying a damn good sing-song. Psychic talent is also a gift that can be enjoyed at all levels, by all types of ordinary people. You don't have to be a fully trained opera singer to enjoy singing and you certainly don't have to be a professional practising clairvoyant or medium to experience psychic phenomena or insight. In no time at all, with a little patience and practice, you too will find that you can do a true psychic tarot card reading. Not only for yourself and friends, but for complete strangers. These readings usually turn out to be much more interesting and successful, not only for the stranger but for you, the budding clairvoyant. Let me guide you through the maze of misinformation, and please take this unique opportunity to learn from my many experiences and mistakes, good, bad or indifferent. But remember when you take up the cards, use your own eyes to see and your own heart to feel, as only you can interpret your own psychic visions and thoughts.

Since it is pure commonsense to start at the beginning, that is what I'll do.

Take up the twenty-two cards that form the major

arcana and select the first card, which should be 'The Fool' or 'Le Mat'. This card is the only one that is not numbered so first we will deal with it in detail, then continue in numerical order.

Lay this card, as you should with all the others that follow, in front of you on a clear table. Systematically study the card. I usually start with the outside edge and work in. But feel free to form a method of your own. Don't just look at the card; study it, get into it. Every little fold of material, every shadow on the ground, even the creases in his or her face will one day prove important to you. As soon as you've studied the card with ordinary vision and feel that you've got the image etched into your brain, close your eyes. Even with your eyes shut, you should still be able to visualize the card. If not, return to it with ordinary vision and then try again until you can create the required image, as I always say, 'At back a ya eyes.' when this is achieved we can go one step further and view the card with psychic vision. Watch the card as it appears at the back of your eyes. Does the card look the same, or is it changing? Maybe the hair looks longer or the face prettier. The image could be trying to tell you that it's female. If the face appears old and withered you could be psychically viewing an older person. Don't just look for facial changes. I have psychically seen and felt this card, as with all the others, twist, change and adapt its basic composition. These weird and wonderful contortions serve to reveal much that has been hidden, past, present and future. Bandage has appeared on the hands when my client or someone close to them has suffered or will suffer a hand injury. The yellow headband appears to glow when there are head problems. The view is not always bad. I once saw the shoes on the fool turn into delicate pink ballet dancing shoes. Then the baton that the fool holds in his right hand changed into a golden chalice. With this psychic view I was able to inform my client that she had a daughter who would soon win an award for ballet dancing. She was more than pleased to hear this as her daughter had been waiting to be accepted into a top dancing school.

When the cards appear to change, or even just blend a

little, you can be sure that your psychic eye is working for you. Psychic viewing is very important but there are many other psychic senses that will now be automatically activated. Emotions play a big part in all readings. Any card in the pack can make me feel happy, sad, lonely, angry, tired, confused, ecstatic, elated, in love, maternal, jealous and so on. Dropping me, without warning, into any one of a thousand other weird or wonderful moods. The psychic ear, once stimulated, will pick up the loud rattlings of a train or the soft whispers of a lover, the spiteful tongue of a rival or the crying of a long waited for baby. So you must be prepared for the sounds that do come from inside your head. Listen whilst you look. And do try not to worry about your destiny becoming similar to that of the ill-fated Joan of Arc. I think they've stopped burning people at the stake now. For the time being anyway.

Time to decide on sensations about you physically. Do you feel hot or cold, wet or dry, flustered, in pain or even sick? These feelings can help you to decide whether the client is in pain or crying with happiness, dancing on a warm beach or walking in freezing rain. All these feelings have to be taken into consideration in order to correctly assess the information that the psychic side of the brain is trying to transmit to you. I know it must sound as if you are going to have to spend the next few years learning how to control these new psychic senses, but this is just not so. You already know how to look, listen and feel. All that you've got to do now is experience those same senses on a much quieter psychic level. Which really only means that you're going to have to listen a little harder, look closer and delve deeper into the bottomless pit of your emotions.

It would be impossible for me to relate to you all the psychic visions that I have experienced through the years. However, as I deal with each card I will try to tell you first of the basic meaning that the card has for me, then of the previous psychic situations that that particular card has transmitted. As I stated previously, we will start with the fool because it is the only card in the pack that is not numbered, then continue in numerical order.

LE MAT (The Fool)

Basic
Obviously, to be a fool. To have little knowledge. To be fooled or to fool others.

Psychic
In a health section I have seen the zig-zag pattern that runs down the leg of the tights open up and reveal both past and future plastic hip operations. In a personality section I have watched as the face has changed to that of my client, then paraded on a stage to reveal that my client's profession was that of an actor. In a wealth section, the little hand with its pointed index finger has waved a positive 'NO' when a client has asked if a future business venture would be successful. Even the lettering at the bottom of the card can help with a reading. There have been times for me when it has glowed, or just appeared to stand out a little more than usual. This frequently happens when I am psychically viewing a person with the name of Lee or Matthew.

I   LE BATELEUR (Magician)

Basic
To be sensitive to the problems of others. To sense spirit world around you. To be a budding medium no less.

Psychic
The chest plate once became transparent and painful broken ribs were freely exposed. I remember one client in particular who really rattled the psychic side of my brain. As I psychically viewed this intriguing picture of the magician, the figure within the card itself took on the appearance of the participating client. Then I saw her lie face down on the table and wriggle her toes over the edge of it. The client informed me that she had spent many months in hospital in that very position to relieve the pain of an injured spine. This card helped me to find a treasured engagement ring that a client mistakenly

thought had been stolen. I patiently watched the card whilst the cup on the table grew and eventually looked like a toilet. Then it settled on the base of the card in front of the draped table-cloth. The drape moved slightly and the glint of gold sparkled from the crevice between the carpet and the wall. Hence one ring successfully found on the floor in the loo and one very happy client.

Gifts have magically appeared from the box on the table to reveal past or future presents of some importance. The hands have looked arthritic and the face has appeared flustered from toothache. I have found this card extremely helpful when studying the health of a client or a close relative.

II *JUNON* (The High Priestess)

Basic
Wisdom, and commonsense. No point in trying to fool this person, is there? Just look at her as she stands there so gracefully, oozing confidence. This card can represent a sister or other female friend. Usually a person who likes to help others but requires little in return.

Psychic
This card contains a peacock and I have found that its appearance in a personality section usually indicates that the client is very good with animals. However, on one occasion the bird changed into a little dog and sank its teeth into the bare leg next to it. As it happened, the woman who sat before me had been wrestling with a heart-rending problem. She didn't know whether to have her dog put to sleep or not, because it had suddenly started to bite and had recently attacked her own grandchild.

III *L'IMPERATRICE* (Empress)

Basic
Action and fertility of the brain as well as the body. Hard work is made to look easy by this person, especially when it

appears in a work set. The card is also known as the 'Earth Mother' so naturally indicates the essence of being a great parent, male or female.

Psychic
My job becomes easy when the empress turns up in the health set, for it almost guarantees that the client is pregnant. Always assuming that the client of course, is female. If good cards surround it, no problem, she's happy. If there are swords with it, there could be complications ahead – sometimes with the child but more often than not with her spouse or living situation. The empress usually turns up in a work set when my client is a workaholic or about to set up some new and exciting business venture.

IIII *L'EMPEREUR* (Emperor)

Basic
The very essence of this card portrays a powerful but lonely and often sad man. The shield that he holds suggests that he is a man of authority, possibly with important letters after his name. A solicitor, lawyer or maybe even a high ranking doctor.

Psychic
The shield itself often reveals to me names that are of interest to the client. Once, when the red on the legs started to run like blood I was given a brief view of what I assumed to be a road accident where the husband of the client was involved. With this information the client promptly took out essential hospital insurance. Within three weeks of acquiring the policy the prediction proved positive! The poor man was trapped beneath a car he had been repairing. He was off work for a number of months and needless to say, the insurance money was more than welcome.

V *JUPITER* (High Priest)

Basic
The male figure portrayed in this card looks a bit fed up, but there's kindness in his face. I find that he usually identifies with a person the client is close to in real life. The client will find he's a good listener or person to listen to. This card often represents a dad but sometimes an older brother or sympathetic male friend.

Psychic
In a travel section the eagle in this card transports me to many countries, but seems to favour Canada. Over the years I've told quite a few delighted clients that they would be emigrating to this fantastic country. In a health set the naked chest of this grand old gentleman has appeared dark from the pain of acid pouring into his gut; acid that may eventually cause painful stomach ulcers.

VI *L'AMOUREUX* (The Lovers)

Basic
Love, harmony and happiness. To have a love of life and nature, but more importantly, to be a lover.

Psychic
Boy, have I had fun with this card! Once, when a very prim and proper looking woman sat before me, full of airs and graces, I very bluntly told her that I could plainly see her with her secret knock off! (Her lover for those amongst you who do not understand the more common classification.) For a few moments she tried to deny the fact. Then she must have thought, 'to hell with it', and asked me if her husband would ever find out.

This sure was some lucky woman. A rich devoted husband and a wealthy boyfriend. She was crafty as well because she made certain that they never, ever met.

Be alert for the very angelic cupid in this card. I have found that any card with an astral manifestation either holds a message from spirit world or predicts a forthcoming death. Close scrutiny of all four figures should enable some sort of identification. Watch to see which figure glows or becomes more apparent, then listen. If there is a message from beyond the veil you will soon know whether it's from someone young, old, male or female. Please be careful, because even loving messages can be exceptionally painful and embarrassing to both the client and the reader.

VII   *LE CHARIOT* (The Chariot)

Basic
There are only two cards in the whole pack that are divided in half, and this is the first. The card to me suggests that there is a 'shall I go or stay' situation. I find the man at the top of the picture rather arrogant and proud. He stands there as if he has conquered all and won, despite all odds.

Psychic
Since the chariot is an ancient form of transport, it's not too surprising that this chariot frequently forms the basis of today's modern car. I've correctly predicted problems with wheels, engines and lights. I do worry when specific technical terms are whispered to me that only a mechanic would understand. However, this only happens when I'm talking to a mechanic. The correct diagnosis of an engine's faults annoy some men and astonish others, but they all have two things in common. They do listen and they do go back and examine their cars, I'm very pleased to say.

VIII   *LA JUSTICE* (Justice)

Basic
Obvious. To acquire justice. To be just. A fighter for truth and a defender of the less fortunate. The scales are symbolic of having the mental capacity to weigh up the pros and cons. The sword gives her the power to cast out evil and set the world right. Can infer that legal dealings are on the way.

Psychic

This card has psychically set me in courtrooms. There I have watched as my client, or a person who the client is involved with, has been sent down or released. The cases and convictions vary but the worry, sadness and frustration doesn't.

When future travel is indicated in a reading, this figure of justice easily adopts the Statue of Liberty pose, so America is never very far away for the client. The head, eyes, and mouth often look painful when I view this card. In fact, I correctly, but sadly, predicted a brain tumour for one unfortunate client.

VIIII   *L'ERMITE* (Hermit)

Basic

To be a hermit, to sit back and watch or rest. A quiet soul who enjoys books and the opportunity to study. Sometimes it can relate to a person who has gone into a shell and hidden from the world.

Psychic

This man holds a lamp, much like Florence Nightingale. The fact that he is male is irrelevant; this is a healer. I remember a vision of him as he soothed away the pains of a child about to undergo major surgery, then comforted and assured the mother that the child would be fine. Once, when I related such a scene to a client, she almost cried with relief because she'd been extremely worried about her only grandson who had been critically ill for days. The walking stick is obviously emphasized when someone in the client's life either is, or will be, using a walking aid. The robe of the hermit can also play quite an informative role. It easily adapts to a surgeon's gown, scholarly cape or a dressing-gown. Just watch and wait as you psychically view. Much will be eventually revealed.

X   *LA ROUE DE FORTUNE* (The Wheel of Fortune)

Basic
Simple. The wheel of fortune is turning, which means that
money could be coming or going. Only psychic viewing
will tell you which way.

Psychic
A strange card, this one, relating to much more than just
money. One girl in the picture is blindfolded and naked.
This figure positively glowed for me the day a young lady
came for a reading. I had to tell her that her future
modelling career would prove unsuccessful if she insisted
on continuing with it blindly. She needed professional
help to put her on a safe and financially secure road. Her
present employer would only exploit her and she knew it.
It was time to move on.

When a client asks me if a forthcoming venture is going
to be successful, I just look at this card and wait to see if I
get the elated feeling of the man on top of the wheel. Then
I can say 'yes, go ahead'. This is not always the case.
Sometimes I relate better to the poor fellow who is falling
off the wheel. When this happens, the client must prepare
for any impending disaster.

XI   *LA FORCE* (Strength)

Basic
Forces; army, navy, airforce, police or fire brigade. Heavy
connections with any type of uniform. Also to be strong or
have strength.

Psychic
This card in a work section has frequently predicted
enlistment into one of the armed forces. In a health set, if
I'm attracted to the eyes or mouth of the lion, I may send
my client to the optician or dentist. The force card freely
turns up when a marriage to a man in uniform is
predicted.

One client was exceptionally pleased when I told her

she would win at a future dog show with her beloved golden labrador. You see, with psychic vision I had seen the lion change nicely into a big yellow dog. Then the club on the floor altered its composition to look like a trophy, suggesting a well-earned win for both dog and owner.

XII   *LE PENDU* (The Hanging Man)

Basic
Well, what sort of a fine old mess has this man got himself into? He's hung himself, so it's obvious that he has given up. He's surrendered to his problems; his whole world is upside down.

Psychic
This card sadly often appears in the personal section when a client has given up on a spouse or child. I have never ever yet found it to be a card that predicts good aspects. It normally turns up as a warning card and often predicts loss of money or esteem. When it's in a health set the spine and neck are places to closely watch, as this card has in the past indicated very serious problems in these areas.

XIII   *LA MORT* (Death)

Basic
I don't think there is a basic for this one. Someone with a bit of insight could possibly write a book on the many meanings and feelings that this card is capable of creating. Nevertheless we have to start somewhere, so here goes. End, change, and inevitably death. A fresh start, a new beginning. A time to put the past behind you and start again.

Psychic
This is a card where you really do have to take into consideration all of your senses. When found in the personality set, if you feel a deep emotional sense of loss, it may well infer that the client has suffered a recent

bereavement. On the other hand, the client could just be a curious person who likes to get to the bones of the matter. When it appears in the home set, it does not necessarily predict the forthcoming death of a person. It may, however, foretell the end of living in a property, merely to move on. Seen in a work section, redundancy, retirement and the sack have to be considered. Don't forget that some people would be happy to pack up work, whilst for others it would be a disaster. The way you feel should help you to predict whether the outcome has good or bad vibes. Never ever disregard your own psychic finer feelings, or the sensitivity of the person that you are reading for. Obviously in a health set the card is warning of a future death, but don't always assume that this will upset the client. I have met quite a few people who have been happy to know that death is just around the corner. These women and men, old and tired themselves, are still responsible for the welfare of their even older and frailer relatives. Many desire death with a little dignity for their aging loved ones and are happy that their suffering and heartache is at last over. On the other hand, I remember quite clearly one cantankerous old woman who came for a reading. She wanted to know exactly how long some poor old man had got to live. Apparently he had been daft enough to propose to her. I say daft, because she openly told me that she was only after his money. She didn't love him and had no intention of looking after him for very long. If he was going to kick the bucket soon, she'd marry him. But if he was going to live for a long time, she wasn't going to bother. I assumed that either there wasn't much money, or she had another ailing candidate in mind. I was pleased to announce that the poor old guy would live to a ripe old age. I even exaggerated – just a little, mind you. Well! Someone had to look after him and he was much better off without that scheming biddy!

XIIII   *TEMPERANCE* (Temperance)

Basic
This for me is a water card as she's pouring wine and there's water in the background. Also the girl appears calm

and patient, suggesting tranquility.

Psychic
Another fun card for me. I've not only been able to predict travel over water, but actually named the country that would eventually be visited. This card made it easy for me to foresee a young girl win many swimming medals and then go on to be a brilliant swimming coach. It has also helped me to predict water problems with the body and a washing-machine.

XV   *LE DIABLE* (Devil)

Basic
A violent card, a sign of trouble, past, present and future. Often associated with a dark devious person whose only ambition in life is to torment others.

Psychic
When the devil is depicted within personality I have to decide whether I have formed an affinity with the crouched child in the card or the devil himself! Some of my clients dislike it when I tell them that the devil is truly themselves. In other words, they have become so involved with the materialistic side of life, that they have forgotten how to love or really live. They are at war with themselves and all around them.

During one psychic reading I felt the pains of being beaten. The woman with me had been unlucky enough to have both a violent father and husband. With common-sense I was able to set her free from her tormentors. She walked from her reading straight into the arms of strangers; people from the welfare and so on. People who would care for her and more importantly, teach her to look after herself.

XVI   *LA MAISON DE DIEU* (The house of God)

Basic
Ruin, setbacks, bankruptcy. Since this is a picture of a building, the buying and selling of property may be on the agenda.

Psychic
Psychic viewing of buildings with this card is almost inevitable. Sometimes I can happily announce, 'Go ahead with your plans and buy with confidence.' Other times I advise to tread with caution. In the health set, if claustrophobic conditions settle around me, I have to decide if the client actually suffers from claustrophobia or is just restricted by life's many day-to-day problems.

XVII   *L'ETOILE* (The Star)

Basic
Hope, satisfaction, good prospects. A little bit of luck on the way.

Psychic
Of all the cards, this one is my own favourite, because I personally identify with it. Clairvoyance is indicated when it appears in the personality pack. In a work section it can reveal that my client is also a practising clairvoyant. When it turns up in wealth, a pools win or some luck is on the way. I told one man that he would win on the pools if he somehow used his daughter's name. He laughed at me. Three weeks later, he won, but he was still annoyed. His daughter had demanded her share of the winnings, and since he had sent his coupon in her name there was little he could do about it. Ah well, you can't win them all!

XVIII   *LA LUNE* (The Moon)

Basic
Caution, danger, error in choosing. A divided card. One

way brings happiness, the other misery. To sit on the fence and not know what to do. To be divided.

Psychic
Now this is quite a peculiar card and has succeeded in putting me in at least one very embarrasing situation. As I looked into the card, I was psychically drawn to the bottom half of the picture. The rest of the illustration slowly disappeared into oblivion. Then the lobster-type creature and the accompanying snail-like friends started to blend and twist until they formed the perfect but bloodless image of a man's very private parts! Now I'm quite used to studying, in detail, any type of psychic vision transmitted, but this was more than a bit embarrassing. For a few moments I was gobsmacked. I then had the humiliating, unthankable task of telling a rather sophisticated woman that her husband was infertile. Well, you should have seen her face. They had been trying for a child for three years and he had been blaming her, saying that she had left it too late and at thirty-two she was too old. It couldn't possibly be him because he had a ten-year-old child from a previous relationship, or so he believed. I'm pleased to say that the marriage did survive this little obstacle. She never did tell him about the reading and with a little bit of, shall we say, inspired creativity, she conceived the child they both desperately needed.

When this card appeared in a health set I correctly predicted that my client needed glasses, as the eyes on the moon seemed to be straining. Another interesting reading was brought about when I found the castle in the background of the picture change and flourish into that of a magnificent grand manor. The man who sat before me was very impressed as he was indeed in the process of restoring an old castle in Spain. This card is extremely intricate with its Romeo and Juliet scene, its dog, tree, doors, figures and veranda. A card where the unexpected should always be expected.

XVIIII   *LE SOLEIL* (The Sun)

Basic
Happiness, contentment and warmth. When the sun
shines love thrives.

Psychic
A very happy card, predicting good vibes from all sources.
The golden circle which surrounds the sun often presents
itself as a wedding ring. In a psychic viewing it slowly
hovers from its position in the sky and gently drifts. It
then shrinks to settle on the book that the depicted lovers
share, promising a good, strong, loving marriage. It's not
only love that thrives under the sun however. Sometimes
it's a symbolic sign that a new business will prove to be
profitable.

XX   *LE JUGEMENT* (Judgement)

Basic
Result, outcome, determination. Something growing,
friends or enemies gathering. As the name suggests, to
receive judgement.

Psychic
Another card with an astral figure, this time with a more
positive attitude. She's either inviting someone to follow
her beyond the veil, or passing on a message from a dear
departed loved one. Whilst reading for one of my older
male clients, his deceased wife sent him a very abrupt
message:
    'Get that bloody chimney swept Sam, before you blow
the flaming house up.'
    Sam's face went white and his eyes almost popped out
of his head. Still in a state of shock he asked me, 'How in
hell's name did you do that? You even sounded like her.'
    I had to admit that I really didn't know how I did it, but
the message was as plain as day. Sam's wife had nagged
him constantly to have the chimney swept from the first
day their gas fire had been installed. Two years after her

death he still hadn't done the job and she was still nagging. Not for much longer though, because Sam made arrangements for a chimney sweep to call as soon as possible.

XXI   *LE MONDE* (The World)

Basic
Change, success, perfection, an unexpected outcome. Travel around the world or knowledge of the world. To think the world of something, or to desire the world.

Psychic
A lovely card this one, which frequently presents itself when I'm dealing with fashion models, film or pop stars. Any person on the right road to success will find this card in a major wealth position during a reading. The strangest vision that I had whilst viewing this card happened recently. The young woman depicted in the card appeared to take the cloth she holds in both hands and drape it over the bull-like beast in the lower half of the picture. Then, in an almost enchanted state, she began to brush the fabric and the beast. When I related this view to her she explained that she had two hobbies. One was grooming and riding horses, the other was designing fabric. The psychic side of my brain had simply tied the two hobbies together and confused me.

These are only a few examples of how the major arcana has worked for me. No two experiences are ever the same, but then again, no two clients are. Although I have only dealt with the major arcana, I wouldn't like you to think that the minor arcana is not as important. Find out how you feel about every card as you set it in front of you, and always be prepared for the totally unexpected.

13   Setting the Cards

Since I have annihilated the whole process and even conception of tarot card readings, I may as well add to my sins and go one step further. As Dad always used to say, 'No point in putting a person on a horse gal, if ya ain't gonna let um ride it.'

So now I will reveal to you my very own original method of laying out the cards. This is one layout that you are never ever going to see used anywhere else, unless that is, you have personally been to see me. Feel free to use it when you first start to read tarot and if it works for you, stick with it. However, you may find that the psyshic side of your own brain will produce a method that will work even better for you, so do experiment a little.

When a client visits me I usually invite them to shuffle the cards for a minute or two. Whilst they do this I like to introduce myself and explain exactly what I can and cannot do, just to clear up any misconceptions and to make the client feel less apprehensive. My little introduction goes something like this:

'I'm going to start by first looking into your personality, home life and work life. Then when you're happy, we'll go off into the future and see what it holds for you. If you have any questions, at any time, please don't hesitate to ask. If I should say anything stupid, like you've got four husbands and sixteen children, feel free to have a go at me, don't stand for any nonsense. I do hear some clairvoyants say that they have one hundred per cent vision. This to me is not only rubbish, but it's dangerous to believe. If I did I'd be doing the pools, and that's fairly obvious. Clairvoyance is a bit like a jigsaw puzzle – you've got some of the pieces and I've got some. If we put them together, we should come up with a decent picture.'

As soon as the client is satisfied that I can indeed see the type of person they are and I do know about their home and work life, we go on into the future. There we look at their health, always important in my readings, and then wealth. Love life along with marriage proposals and children usually feature next. Career prospects, especially for the self-employed, take up a large part of the reading. The last part of the reading frequently reveals the totally unexpected.

The whole pack of cards is then placed on the table and I ask the client to cut them into two small separate stacks of cards, using their left hand. There are supposed to be three reasons for using the left hand:

1. The left hand is evil and will give you away.
2. The left hand leads straight to the heart, so you should get a good reading.
3. The right hand is over-trained and therefore eliminates the essential element of chance.

I prefer the latter but you should, as always please yourself. I then pick up the stack of cards that were originally at the bottom of the pack and proceed to set them out. I place the first card down in what will eventually be a trio of cards – and should reveal the personality of the client. The second card is placed next to it, leaving a little room for psychic insight. This section deals with any aspect about home life. The third card is set likewise. The three cards that end up here expose work modes and attitudes. You should now have three cards in a row, with a little space in-between. Card four, a health card, should be set below and slightly in. Next to this the fifth card, an all important wealth indicator, will rest. Now place another card under the health card but slightly out. This section will eventually relate to the main problem that the client has. The next two cards are for the surprises that life always has in store for us.

So now you should have eight single cards set in front of you: a row of three, then a row of two, and another row of three; eight cards in all. Now repeat the process. The ninth card on top of the first card, the tenth card on top of the second card and so on. You now have sixteen cards, all set in pairs. Repeat the action just once more until you have eight sets of three; twenty-four cards in all. At this stage in the game don't worry too much about remembering the meanings of all twenty-four cards. Brains are just like computers, put too much in too fast and the end result is a brainstorm or a computer error and a flaming disaster if you ain't got a back-up tape or disc. You'll forget much more than you'll remember.

Start with the first three cards that are in the personality set. To begin with, decide how you feel about them as a whole, all together. Are they warm, good cards that insinuate a friendly and happy disposition? Or are they a bit mixed up? Say one card's the king of swords, one's the two of chalices and the other something from the major arcana, like the moon. This type of trio could infer a mixed-up, confused character. Psychically you are going to have to decide whether it's a permanent or temporary condition. Now take each card in turn. Since the king of swords is on the top one may assume that the particular lady is mixed up, because the man in her life is causing her some concern. The two of chalices may be a time link – two years or two months. The moon at the back insinuates that the lady is at the stage of choosing. Will she stay or go? Psychically view the cards once more to make sure that you haven't missed something important. The two of chalices may be presented to you yet again, this time with a totally different meaning. As you visualize it, the two cups in the picture could easily change to two little heads. This could be children who will have to be considered if the client is about to leave the matrimonial home. See what I mean? One card with a single basic meaning but capable of arousing a thousand psychic feelings, visions and thoughts.

Limit yourself on the amount of time you spend in each section or you may become bogged down with petty data. For instance, it's not important that the client is given the relevant ages of the children. It should be enough that you have seen that there are specifically two children who have to be considered before she makes her decision.

Continue with the next set of cards in the same way that

you have dealt with the personality, only adapt your attitude towards a home mood. If there are lots of chalices in this set, the home should be happy. If there are many swords, look for any type of personal or financial problems. When there's a multitude of coins, or pentacles as some call them, there's a suggestion of being unsettled. The client could have just moved or be on the move. Batons for me are always associated with cash. So when these appear I make some sort of effort to see if the client is working from home. Then there's always the possibility that the house has only been bought as a financial asset, a business venture.

Each and every set of three cards should be assessed in an identical manner. Take your time and don't try to do too much too soon. If you are about to become the world's most talented clairvoyant, believe me, the world will wait till you've got it nearly right!

This type of reading, which includes health, wealth and so on, is ideal when you want to impress friends or clients, and there's no shortage of time to gather the vast range of relevant psychic information made readily available. However, there are times in everyone's life when all that's desired is an answer to a question, such as, 'Does this man truly love me?' or, 'Will marriage to this woman bring happiness?'. People on the verge of selling or buying a house, want to know, 'Will my house sell soon?' or even 'Is the price too high?' If you've recently applied for a new position at work, naturally you will ask, 'Is the job going to be mine?' Now there's no reason on earth why you should not acquire just a little psychic insight in order to enhance your own personal life, no matter what the question is. But for this you are going to need a much quicker, less intricate type of reading. The best way to achieve a direct answer is by using a method similar to the following, whereby you will eventually end up psychically viewing five cards only. As always, select a time when you know that you will not be disturbed. Tuning into psychic power is very difficult, though not impossible, in a noisy situation. I also find bright lights very distracting. Calmly sit at a table, pick up the cards and start to shuffle. This is not as easy as it sounds as the tarot cards are much larger than ordinary playing cards. Whilst moving the cards back and forth, think of the question you are about to ask. Keep the question simple and don't make it double-headed, such as, 'Will I pass my exams or not?' Consider all possible outcomes, results or avenues as the cards pass freely and gently over and over in your hands, and wait. Patiently word your question, again and again until a comfortable harmony is produced, each movement of the cards tallying with your query in a sing-song or nursery rhyme manner. When the cards resist movement or stick a little, that's the time to stop. Place the cards face down on the table, then cut them with the left hand into separate piles. Continue to recite your question at all times. Take the stack of cards that would have been at the base of the deck and start to deal them, in a straight line, face down. Place the first card on the table, then put the second card next to it. Now with the third card, cover the second. Put the fourth card on its own next to them. The fifth card is then set down and covered by the sixth. The seventh and last card is positioned alone but against the fifth and sixth. You should now have a row of cards consisting of one on its own, two together, one in the middle on its own, then two more together and finally one single card. Now turn the three single cards face up and then the two pairs of cards, to reveal the face of the base card only. These should be placed below the three single cards and slightly in. You should now be able to see the face of five cards. Within these five cards you will find both answer and question. As an example, I'm going to start with something really simple. Imagine that a young woman wants to know if she's pregnant or not, either because it's too early to tell or because there have been quite a few false alarms. The single cards she turns over reveal the six of swords, the Empress and the seven coins, usually called pentacles. Below are the knave of batons sometimes called rods and the king of swords. The basic meaning for me is as follows. The six of swords is a sexual card. The Empress, often referred to as Mother Earth is a fertility symbol, the seven of coins is a gift of some kind. So I would be very happy to say that sexual activity during a fertile period had produced the gift of a child. Not only that, but because the two base cards are male, it would be fairly safe to announce the birth of a boy. A straight answer to a straight question. Yes she is pregnant. A combination of cards like this would be a classic, and as such require very little psychic viewing because the cards themselves have done most of the work for you. Be that as it may, you should never neglect to view them physically if you want all the information available. Psychic viewing of these cards could bring to light all sorts of complications. There could be a warning against working too hard, the threat of a miscarriage, or even twins. If you desire all the information, you're still going to have to psychically look into the cards, even if the answer appears blatantly transparent.

Let's try another reading, this time a little more complicated. Someone wants to know if they are going to get the promotion they've been after. The cards have been shuffled, cut and set as before. The four of batons, ace of swords and the Chariot. Beneath are the Hermit and the two of batons. The basic meaning for me is this. The four of batons is a labour card and the ace of swords a proposition in business. The Chariot, a divided card, has many basic meanings – To travel, to sit on the fence, or maybe to succeed. For the time being it's far from obvious exactly what this card is trying to tell us.

The Hermit also brings complications as it could mean a variety of things – to sit back and rest or maybe to study the situation first or even give up and hide. Then we have the two of batons, an extremely cryptic card for me. Sometimes it states a time or date, often it means to remarry or revalue the situation. But more often than not, it means you get two bites at the cherry; there are two ways out.

The cards have indeed repeated the question with the first two cards. The four of batons – to labour, and the ace of swords – a proposition at work. Now we have to psychically view the Chariot, first alone, then as part of the whole set. If the man depicted at the top of the card appears triumphant and remains still, we could assume three things.

A. The client will stay in their particular work environment because the man in the card remained still.

B. The job will be offered, the victorious attitude providing this insight.
C. It's fairly obvious the job will be accepted.

Now study the Hermit. Does he appear relaxed? If so, it may mean there was no competition anyway, the job was already in the bag. If however, this figure looks worried and books appear around him, we should suspect that all is not well. Perhaps the job is still heading in the client's direction but more work, research and study is going to be required before a promotion is achieved.

The two of batons would then seem to emphasize this fact, stating yet again that there's still time to brush up on any research. This would enable a person to present a more confident and acceptable character.

So, my answer to this question would be yes, but much depends on your own perception whilst psychically viewing the cards. With one view the promotion was available without trying. The other aspect tended to insinuate that although promotion was possible, much more work and research would be required, and it could take longer than expected.

This method of reading the cards is simple, quick, and as I've said, perfect for a straight yes or no answer. Even the basic meaning of the cards will help you with your quest, but spend a few minutes more and the results will amaze you. With practice, viewing the cards psychically in your head, produces an effective and reliable outlook on any aspect that would normally be 'in the unforseeable future'.

The tarot cards and I have formed a working relationship which helps me to provide my clients with a fast, efficient and accurate reading. I respect and value their assistance. Nevertheless, it's very important to realize that psychic ability or skill is a natural produce of the brain, and not every brain will relate to the cards. This is why there are so many different types of psychics about. Some use a crystal ball whilst others use tea-leaves, sands, rune stones or palms. Each person has to find the method that works best for them, and allows the psychic side of the brain to work freely and efficiently. So formulate your own method, familiarize yourself with the style, then practice like hell.

Don't let anyone tell you your method is wrong because what works for them won't necessarily work for you and vice versa.

14   Is It You?

I now intend to tell you about some of the more interesting and sometimes intriguing cases that I have been involved with.

At this stage in the game, if you are one of my many clients, you may be just a little worried that I have had the audacity to include your particular and often very personal consultation within the forthcoming pages. Please, please, don't hit the panic button yet. I assure you, as with all good stories, I have changed the names to protect the innocent! So unless you tell the world that you are the central figure in one of my compositions, no one but no one, I promise you, will ever know that it's your story.

15   Lady of the Law

Over the years I have seen thousands of clients and many have become frequent visitors. My clientele includes a vast range of professional and intelligent people who are quite able and more than prepared to clinically analyse the contents and value of a clairvoyant reading. Such a client was my barrister, who turned up for a reading on a cold winter's day. This lady, and she was a lady in the true sense of the word, was in her late fifties. The most distinguishing feature about her was her voice. It was like listening to an excited, educated, and intriguing child. How she ever managed to become a barrister I shall never know, for her face radiated more love and understanding than you would expect from the average war-torn, defender of law and order. But a barrister she was, and, it appears, a good one.

As soon as she walked into my reading room, all my psychic senses started to work overtime. My psychic ear began to groan and my stomach tried to do a double somersault, rendering me speechless for a few moments. I regained my composure and tried to pretend that nothing had happened. The cards were then shuffled, cut and placed on the table. This was when I told her she was a defender of the law, which was easy for me to see as the cards had kindly presented her as the justice card within the layout depicting work. I must admit the word 'barrister' didn't spring to mind, but she was suitably impressed. I tried to continue with the reading, but the groan in my ear had now become the unmistakable rumblings of a train. And the sickness in my stomach made the journey final and ... fatal.

The psychic side of my brain was now at war with the

commonsense branch. One team was saying, 'Go on, tell her. She's going to kick the bucket if she catches that train.' Then the other side advised, 'Now look here Kris, you're talking to a barrister. If you're wrong and she misses an important appointment, there's a strong possibility, with your luck, that they could bring back burning witches and clairvoyants at the stake.'

It was time to use a little tact. I needed to sort out my thoughts, so I dabbled with the reading. Her health wasn't as good as it could have been. Her love life was, shall we say, interesting. Then the career section positively declared that if I didn't get my finger out, there wasn't going to be any future for her. So damn it, I was going to have to tell her. I nervously approached the subject, asking her if she was about to travel by train in the very near future. The reply quite shook me.

'You are the clairvoyant, you tell me.'

After rattling that answer around my brain a couple of times, I decided to be more positive.

'You are going on a train journey within the next three days,' I said with a vengeance. Then I continued, 'If you go on that train, you will not return.'

She looked at me a little cynically. 'Why?' she asked. 'Is it a one-way ticket, or will the train crash?'

I looked deeper into the cards for the help and insight that I needed to predict the impending disaster. My psychic senses however, had drawn the line. All the information that I needed to prevent this person's death had been presented to me like a drama on a stage. Now the curtains had been drawn, I knew all I needed to know. So all I had to do was convince her!

I really felt that this woman's fate was to see me in order to prevent her untimely death. So it was vital she understood precisely what I was saying, even if it sounded cruel.

'There is no one-way ticket,' I said, 'and no crash, just a feeling. A feeling that if you go on that specific journey, your life will have completed its circle, and you ... will die.'

Five foot eight inches of immaculately-dressed barrister rose gracefully from the chair, bringing the reading to a premature and abrupt end. She was clearly not amused. I mentally checked my wardrobe for the asbestos evening wear and underwear I might be requiring in the immediate future for any impending barbecue. Anyone for a Winnie the Witch kebab!

She left the house and I watched as she walked to her expensive Mercedes. I couldn't help but wonder why anyone would want to travel by train when they had free access to the sleek and powerful beauty of a Mercedes! Still, such are the ways of the unpredictable wealthy, and who am I to cast aspersions on someone who was evidently a very successful woman? I didn't expect to see or hear from her again, for more than obvious reasons, but I was wrong.

Less than five days later, her unmistakable voice, trickled down the phone line.

'Hello Kris,' she said, 'it's me, the lady you saw last week. The barrister, remember?'

Oh, I remembered all right. It's not every day that I experience death for a client.

'Yes, I remember you clearly,' I said. 'You weren't too pleased with your reading, as I recall. I certainly didn't expect to hear from you this soon.'

'Yes, that's one reason why I'm phoning. To apologize, and to say thank you. You see, you were right. I would have been travelling, by train, the very next day. Actually I was quite looking forward to it, until your warning. I was going to see my sister in London for a few days. However, I phoned her and told her I had toothache. This was a little white lie, but she would have worried if I had gone into detail. So once again, thank you and I'll be seeing you soon.'

She was just about to put the phone down, when I said, 'Hey, hang on a moment. You haven't told me what happened, or why you're thanking me. I'm totally in the dark, please put me out of my misery, or I shall never sleep tonight.'

'Sorry,' she said. 'Thought you would know, being clairvoyant and all that. It was the bombs you know, the bombs that went off in Harrods.' I was still confused and she sensed it. 'My sister and I usually buy all our

Christmas gifts at Harrods. We normally make a day of it, even eating there. It's a treat for both of us. Anyway, because of my imaginary toothache, or rather your prediction, neither of us were in the shop at the time when the bombs went off. As you know, both of us have a serious heart complaint. Even if we hadn't been in the main blast, the ensuing turmoil would have been quite dangerous for us. So once again Kris, thank you.'

I told her I was glad to have helped and would be more than happy to see her again. With that I put the phone down, went through to my husband, and related the whole story to him.

The next time I saw this lady she was very confused and a little frightened. She was under the impression that she had cheated death and that there must be some sort of penalty to pay. It took me ages to make it clear to her that her destiny was to see me first and so avoid an early death. This way, she would also be able to help those who needed her particular talents. It was then I told her that a tree does not die if you cut off one of its damaged branches. It just keeps growing and developing many other branches that often bear much sweeter fruit. One of her branches had been pruned. Now it was up to her to keep growing, to continue with her life and enjoy the fruits of her labours. For a few years yet, anyway.

16   Divided Loyalties

I wish I had had as much success with the young man who decided, under pressure, to have a go at a clairvoyant consultation. He arrived for his reading precisely on time, eight o'clock on the dot. There he stood at the door with his crash helmet under his arm, struggling to remove his gauntlet-type gloves. He was a big fellow, about six foot two and ruggedly handsome. His eyes were almost as black as his shoulder-length curly hair. He was a looker all right, and he knew it. I had a sneaky feeling that this guy could charm the birds from the trees.

I invited him in out of the cold and asked him to follow me to the reading room. He hesitated for a moment, looking at his damp and somewhat dirty boots. I assured him that the carpet had seen much worse in the past, so there was no need to worry about marking it. Anyway, I was well and truly overdue for a new carpet.

Taking off his leather jacket, he relaxed in the chair opposite me, so I began the reading. Even before the last card dropped into place, an immense sense of doom settled silently around me, like a great cascade of gigantic snowflakes from above. The longer I sat there, the colder I became. This was about to be one of my most difficult, unhappy and useless readings.

Disregarding any foreboding that I had, I started the reading as I always do, with a little about his past and present. This part was easy. I told him about his wife and kids, his bike, car and job. Then I thoroughly rattled him by describing the other woman in his life ... his mistress. For one brief moment his face registered unbelievable shock, either at the bluntness of my statement (that he had a knock off), or at the realization that this stranger, looking straight at him, was actually able to see any, or maybe even all, of his indiscretions! Talk about the eternal triangle – this was a man who loved and needed both of these women in his life. I sincerely hoped that this was the problem that had succeeded in giving me the shivers at the beginning of the reading. To say the least, he was surprised to find me so positive, and asked me if I was always so direct. He smiled when I told him I had a reputation for not pussyfooting around to maintain.

Then, patiently, I waited for my psychic senses to relax, expecting the tenseness and the chill that surrounded me to disappear. It usually did, once the main problem had been revealed. However, this was not to be. My heart-beat slowed down, then my arms and legs seemed to increase in weight. My vision alternated between darkness then exceptional clarity. This man's life was fast coming to an end. I had to decide not only if I was going to tell him, but whether that knowledge would do any good, or just add to his problems.

I took a good look at his face. There was a sadness about his eyes. He was much too young to die, but I had a feeling that he knew he was going to. Then, from the back of my brain, I heard the all-too-familiar voice of my friend from the desert, softly whispering.

'Tell him Kris, he needs to know, tell him.'

So there it was, I had to tell him, but my friend from the desert (who I had recently christened Psy, short for psychic) forgot to mention whether it would do any bloody good. I approached the subject with a great deal of care and mental deliberation.

'I believe you are putting your life in grave danger,' I said. 'I'm sorry, but I sense death all about you. Please, please, give me a little time, then I'll try to find out why, when, and where. Then perhaps, God willing, your life will continue.'

I expected him to look disturbed, or laugh or just disbelieve me, but this time it was his turn to shake me.

'I'm here, because I believe I'm going to die.' Slowly, almost painfully he continued. 'I can't plan for next year. My thoughts won't settle on anything nice or interesting that should be to come. Like holidays, swapping the bike

or changing this flaming job. I can't even see myself
choosing between the two women. All my life I've enjoyed
plotting and planning, anything and everything. Now it's
as if there's a massive wall that's blocking my every
thought. I sit down determined to plan for next year, but
the brain won't stick with what I want to plan. My thoughts
constantly roll towards making a will. Then I actually plan
my funeral, and would you believe I wonder if my kids will
be all right with a new dad? I don't know, am I going crazy
Kris, am I?'

I silently waited for him to calm down, then I said,
'You're not going mad love, just a little psychic, and now
that you're here, there's a chance that, together, we can get
you through this period and you'll live to be a crotchety old
man.'

With that he relaxed a little, and I prepared myself for the
forthcoming ordeal. With closed eyes, I mentally searched
my brain for the familiar, deep, dark abyss that usually
holds all the answers. I needed to know when, where and
why he was going to die, if I was going to help him at all.
The darkness swallowed me up. I could feel the damp
rough wall as I walked deeper and deeper into this mental
chasm. I had to know, I just had to. Slowly I continued my
journey into the depths of the unknown, waiting for that
pin-point of revealing light. Suddenly it was there, like a
flickering candle. Then it grew bigger and brighter; my
journey was almost complete. All I had to do now … was
watch and wait.

The sun rolled in a great arch over my head. Then the
moon that followed remained high in the sky, so it was
very late at night. Rain fell all around me, making me cold
and wet. My feet, bare as always, felt the puddles of water
swish about my toes. There was no time to marvel at my
arrival, for there in the distance, I saw a bike, his bike,
cutting easily through the rain. Closer and closer it came,
the noise of the engine becoming louder. Then when he
was about twenty feet away from me, he lost control, his
bike swerved, leaving the road and landing in the
hedgerow. No big crash or sparks, just a sickening thud.
The wheels were still spinning. I knew even then that his
heart had stopped, because the pounding of my own heart

was now almost silent.

This is quite normal for me. When my client feels pain or sadness, so do I. At that moment, I could feel the life and soul ebbing from the body of this young man, ready and eager to meet its maker. My mind was in the same turmoil as his was at the time of the accident. He was changing partners, yet again swapping from girlfriend to wife, or vice versa. Not really knowing who he wanted to be with, or why. Literally torn between the two. So, now I had all the answers. When? On a dark, cold, wet winter's night, and soon. Where? On a lonely country lane. Then the why? Because he was changing partners yet again. I related all this to him, every little detail. All he had to do was stay with the woman he was with, whoever it was. Then, as an added precaution, not to even consider using his bike late at night, especially if it was raining. If he followed that advice, just for a couple of months, he could have gone on to live and enjoy his life, but no. All the information in the world didn't help. He took that last fatal journey less than four weeks later. It was so sad; such a waste of life.

I found out later that he had told his wife and girlfriend about the reading. They had both pleaded with him not to travel at night on the bike. They had begged him to use the car. When they visited me to thank me for trying to help (even though it had proved to be useless), they told me that he loved his bike as much as he loved his women. They both desperately loved him, despite his philandering ways. I now believe that he had to take that last ride on his beloved bike, purely because he couldn't and wouldn't choose between the two women. He loved them both too much. Enough to die for them....

17   Sneinton Case

Just before Christmas 1985, very early in the morning and with a shred of annoyance in my voice, I answered a persistently ringing phone. A faint, frail voice at the other end urgently said, 'Mum says will you come now, she must see you.'

With that the phone went dead. Now as a rule I don't worry too much about strange calls. In my profession you get them all the time. Anything from, 'Is it going to rain next Friday and spoil our cricket match?' to, 'Will the spirit that keeps making love to me make me pregnant?' I advise when and if I can, but there's a fair share of annoying crank calls. This little girl's particular message rattled me however, and all that day I waited for her to phone again, hoping that I would be able to help her.

Mid-afternoon she phoned again. This time I was able to get her name and address, but she was still unable or unwilling to tell me why her mum wanted to see me. Nevertheless, I assured a breathless, tearful young lady that I would be with her mum as soon as possible. My husband drove me to the Sneinton address I had been given although he was still a bit concerned that we were out on a wild goose chase. But he was a sucker for kids and knew that neither of us would get any peace until we had at least made some sort of effort to help a child who sounded so desperate.

When I arrived at the address, I was almost dragged into the front room of the large terraced house. There before me, in an old armchair, sat a woman. One of her legs was encased in a vast amount of plaster. This she was resting on a small stool. Her face was as grey as ash. Her eyes were so full of misery that I could feel her torture eat at my very soul. She was obviously in a great deal of mental and physical pain.

Apparently her husband, who fifteen months previously had lost his self-respect along with a very demanding job, had been missing for about three weeks. The man she loved, worshipped even, had got up early one morning, wrapped all the kids' Christmas presents, then lovingly put them under the decorated tree. All of his valuables and insurance policies had been carefully placed on the table, but no message. Nothing to say why or where he had gone. His wife, Pauline, was devastated and so were his three devoted children.

The police had been called, but they couldn't help. The Salvation Army weren't having much luck either. However, a young police constable had suggested that, as a last resort only, Pauline should contact me. He had heard via his wife that I was quite good, which could have been a compliment if he hadn't been in such a hurry to vacate the premises. I'm not saying that he didn't care – just that since there was nothing more he could really do, he wanted to get home, which is only natural.

Pauline had broken her leg five days previously. She had been cleaning the bedrooms, doing anything to keep her mind busy and to stop her crying, especially in front of the children, when she heard the front door open. She ran across the landing to the top of the stairs. She was sure it was her husband returning. In her haste, she slipped, falling down most of the stairs, almost knocking herself unconscious and inevitably, breaking her leg.

There was no one at the door. It had mysteriously opened and half closed itself. This could easily have been the wind, but for Pauline it was the last straw. The opening and closing of that door was a bad omen to her. She was now quite certain that Brian was dead. She had given up all hope of him returning to her ... alive, and now she wanted me to contact him in the spirit world!

I listened to her story. Then I had to tell her that I was a clairvoyant who looked into the future, not a medium who spoke to those who had passed on into spirit. She was so disappointed; I felt such a toad. She begged me to try to contact him, and then out of the blue something or someone at the back of my mind said, 'Come on Kris, get off your backside, you know you can do it.' It was Psy, the man from my dream desert, interfering with my stream of thoughts, just to let me know that he was there to help. It was now easy to give in to Pauline's pleas. I asked for a photo of her husband, which she hastily rustled up from the bottom of her handbag. I held his photo, then sat back in the comfortable armchair and closed my eyes. I didn't know what to expect so I just let my mind relax and take me where it wanted to go. Free of the physical body, I soon found I was in the all-too-familiar chasm that my mind usually steps into just before I go forward in time. This is not the same approach as when I visit spirit world.

I walked deeper and deeper into the darkness, waiting for the flashes of light that I knew would reveal the truth. Suddenly I could hear a heart-beat, then I saw a motorway sign giving directions for Birmingham. This soon disappeared and the name Hull became bigger and brighter.

I looked at Pauline and said, 'Well love, he's not dead, so I can't contact him in spirit world.' I could see she didn't believe me, so I carried on. 'First of all I think he's heading for Birmingham, but wait a minute, Hull's becoming more prominent.'

The word Hull triggered off a reaction. She now looked more than a little interested. I returned to my resting position and once again stepped into the unknown.

'I can see him now with an old battered suitcase, at this door. It's a cold Valentine's day and he's grown a beard. There's a black and silver motorbike just outside the door. It's in such poor condition that it shouldn't be on the road at all. He's cold, tired and hungry, but he's back. Not to stay, I must add, because he's found work and somewhere to live. Brian needs his family and he truly loves you, but full-time work and the respect it brings is essential to him. He's going to ask you to sacrifice all that you have now, your nice home and all your friends in Nottingham, to live in a run down dilapidated ruin of a property in Hull. And you know something, there's nothing more certain than the fact that you will go. It'll be hard to start with, but there's real happiness again for the whole family, in the not too distant future.

If Pauline could have got up, she would have danced with joy. She couldn't tell me fast enough that Brian had started to grow a beard just before he had gone missing. He loved motorbikes and it would be nothing unusual for him to turn up with an old unroadworthy one. Then Hull was the only place that he had any friends or family connections. The police had looked there but had not been able to find him. Pauline didn't need any more convincing. Nevertheless, I went on to tell her about the future she would share with her husband as soon as he sorted himself out. The only reason that he had disappeared in the first place was because he was sure that the family would be better off without him. He had had no luck finding a job and was disgusted with himself. Being a proud man, he found it hard to approach the D.H.S.S. Then in a very depressed state he had decided to end it all. But when it came to the crunch, he couldn't. So he just ... disappeared, feeling even more of a failure.

When I left, my client was in a much happier frame of mind, even though she knew that she would not be seeing her husband until the second week in February. She asked if she could phone me if she felt down. Since I knew there were going to be quite a few down days I told her to call me whenever she needed her morale boosting.

Pauline phoned me many times. Again and again I had to assure her that he would come home – she just had to sit tight. I was confident that he would return just as I had seen him. So when 14 February came and there was no sign of him, even I began to panic. Pauline was on the phone every hour. Then at eleven o'clock that night she called once more, this time with good news. He had not returned yet, but he was on his way. He had phoned to tell her that his bike had broken down on the motorway and he would be with her in about two hours. He was sorry; he would explain to her later why he had gone missing. In the meantime he loved her as much as ever and told her not to lock up until he got back.

I met Pauline and Brian for a drink a few months later. By this time they had solved many of their problems. Brian was dying to meet me, still finding it hard to believe that I could follow him so easily and with so much detail.

'The only time you confused me,' I told him, 'was when you went to Birmingham first, then Hull after. No one in their right mind travels to Hull via Birmingham.'

Brian smiled, then told me that he had, in fact, got on the first train that had come into the station. This was the train to Birmingham. However, he lost his nerve, got off, and then wandered round the station for another hour. Still sure that the family he loved would be better off without him, he caught the next train and that one was heading towards Hull.

We all had a great night. Brian said that no matter what the future held, he would never leave Pauline again. (Especially since she had her own tuned-in bloodhound, who was more than able to find him, wherever he was.) I warned Brian jokingly that I didn't like the idea of being referred to as bloodhound, but if he did go walkabout again, he would find out that my bite was a damn sight more painful than my bark. We said goodbye and went our own ways. I was certain that this couple would have many happy years together. They deserved a little happiness. Recently Pauline came to see me and let me know that they were still together and that the despair of five years ago was almost forgotten. They were about to start a new business and looking forward to a happy, busy and prosperous new year.

18   Men, Sceptical Men

This story is also about a couple; only this time, to improve their lives, I had to split them.

I was out on a party booking for about six people, somewhere in Long Eaton. I remember the welcome being as warm as the old corner house itself. No one had to be clairvoyant to see that four of my clients were in fact sisters. All of them had pretty pale blue eyes and fine curly hair, now in various shades of grey, due to the fact that they were all in their fifties and sixties. The other two women were a lot younger, and turned out to be the daughters of one of the sisters. One other person was present, a woman I didn't have the pleasure of reading for. She was much older than the rest of the group and turned out to be the grandma of the younger women and obviously the mother of the older women. She was well over eighty and sat in what was unmistakably her chair, close to the fire. When I asked her if I would be reading her cards she bluntly told me, 'If the future holds any surprises for me at eighty-seven, I don't want to know.' She smiled sweetly, knowing that she had at least voiced her disapproval, then returned her attention to the television programme she was watching. After the initial introductions, I was led to a quieter room, just across the passage, away from the lounge where they all gathered. I didn't need my psychic senses to send me back in time – this room did that all on its own. It was in a time warp; nothing had been changed for over ninety years.

I sat at a dark oak table with matching carved chairs. The seats had been covered with a rich tapestry fabric. Heavy dark green velvet curtains toned beautifully with the thick Axminster carpet and the polished wood-panelled walls were clearly original and well cared for. A real coal fire crackled from a small cast-iron grate. A variety of brass ornaments surrounded the fireplace. On the floor was a brass and wood fender, along with the traditional companion set, comprising of a small poker, brush and dustpan. I was in heaven! Never had I ever been so at home. The readings tonight, in this atmosphere, just had to be good, and so they were.

My psychic senses were as sharp as a razor. This made all the readings quick and easy. The clients were as much impressed with my psychic ability as I was. All too soon I'd finished, then regrettably, I had to leave this fantastic room. I was invited to join the party and given a drink whilst I waited for my husband to collect me at ten o'clock. It was then that I was told that the room I had been reading in had not been changed since Grandad had died, more than forty years ago. He had brought most of his treasured furniture from his own home, which he had been forced to sell many years ago. Now no one used the room finding it (unlike me) uncomfortable and cold. Since there was no shortage of space in the house, the room had remained as a shrine to Grandad.

We were all happily chatting away when the doorbell rang. The atmosphere immediately changed, all of them becoming quieter. Then the door opened and a stout man entered. He had come for his wife and laughingly asked if we had all had enough spirits, or was there any whisky left for him. The hostess quickly got him a drink and he then turned his attention towards me.

'So, you're the lassie who claims to be able to look into the future are you?' There was the unmistakable note of contempt in his voice. Since I hadn't had time to assess him, I smiled meekly at him, allowing him to continue voicing his all too condemning opinion. 'You know,' he said, 'I've met people like you before, and no one has been able to prove to me that they can see into the future, or talk to the dead.' There was no stopping him now. The chatty, friendly crowd had become a quiet, almost scared, captive audience for him. 'All that you have lassie,' he sarcastically informed me, 'is a gift for the gab.'

My efforts to get a word in edgeways were totally

ignored. I had no choice but to let him carry on. 'Now, if you could tell me one true fact about me that you haven't learned from my wife, or the others, I may, just may, think twice, lassie. Not something wishy-washy mind you, something positive. Now lassie, come on, let's see what you can do.'

The irresistible desire to bark and bite this man's head off at the same time was becoming more than apparent. I had held my tongue long enough, so I let him have it with both barrels.

'OK, give me a minute,' I said. How I longed for the help and serenity of Grandad's room now. I looked deep into his head, wondering if I could cut this arrogant man down to size without causing his poor dominated wife any more trouble.

'Why are you staring at me? Lassie, are you stuck? Can't you reveal any of my dark secrets?' He stood there, laughing, not only at me, but at the other women present.

'I'm looking into your head,' I said slowly, 'to see if there's anything there, but I'm not having much luck.' This made one of the women laugh a little nervously.

I sat in one of the large comfortable chairs knowing the first thing I'd got to do was calm my irritated temper. Then I closed my eyes and ears in order to isolate myself from the now disruptive atmosphere. It was difficult at first to obtain the depth of darkness needed to psychically view this obnoxious person. Placing the cool palms of my hands over my closed eyes intensified the level of concentration and produced the desired result. Bingo! Psychic vision in glorious technicolour. I silently watched as the dream-like pictures rolled around my head. I knew I'd see Mr Oh So Arrogant, but I certainly didn't expect to find him stark naked, struggling to get into one of those old-fashioned, lace up corsets. The contortions of this extremely large, vain man, rendered me unable to hold the psychic state for more than a few seconds. But that didn't matter – his secret was out – and boy was it a corker.

'Ah, now I can see your secret.' I waited. If I was going to reveal this fact, I was going to do it with a little panache. He defiantly looked at me, daring me to say something. 'Well, if you're sure,' I hesitated, but he had asked for it.

'Well, my dear, I know you wear a corset. Is that proof enough?'

His wife went white while he turned a peculiar shade of red, then an outrageous purple, as he tried to spit out his words.

'She told you, that cow told you!' he said, as he tried to cross the room to get to his wife, who was already hiding behind one of her sisters. I stopped him – he wasn't that much bigger than me. Then I had to shout at him two or three times.

'No she didn't, she damn well didn't, I tell you. She's too much of a lady to reveal any of your weaknesses, especially this one, and know that.' Two of the women had hustled the wife into another room, whilst the rest of them stood defiantly barring the door. Knowing I had a back-up team, I verbally attacked him again before he had time to recover from the first onslaught. 'It's high time you started to appreciate that wife of yours, before someone comes along and treats her with just one ounce of respect, and then steals her from under your very nose. Then you will have lost not only the woman that you love, but your cook, cleaner and bookkeeper.' By now he had gone pale and quiet – it was time to smooth a few ruffled feathers. 'Look, imagine how you would feel if she was in someone else's arms. There's many a man out there who would give his right arm for a little treasure like her, but it's you she loves. God in heaven knows why, but she does.'

He turned away from me, then hastily disappeared through the same door that he had entered only twenty minutes previously, leaving us all in a stunned silence. I felt a little sorry for him then, but it was too late. I had said my piece, only to regret it, even if it was true.

I turned to face the other women in the room, expecting them to ask me to leave there and then. But the old lady suddenly said, 'Someone get that girl a drink, she needs it. Well done lass, I only wish I'd have said exactly the same ten years ago!'

So instead of being thrown out into the night, we actually celebrated the fact that a bully had been put in his place. When we discussed the possible consequences of my dramatic announcement, I was told not to worry about his wife because they would make sure she was well cared for. One of the sisters confided in me.

'That man has been treating my sister like dirt for years. We've tried to get her to leave him, but all she says is, she loves him. They did have a good marriage till the children left home, then he changed. It's true he's a bully, but he's never hurt her physically. He gets his kicks from tormenting her mentally. His words are often more painful than a slap in the face. Let's hope that after tonight, he'll treat her better or she will find the guts to leave him.'

There was a knock at the door – this time it was my husband. As we said our goodbyes, they told me yet again not to worry about their sister, and assured me that they would let me know what the outcome was.

Weeks later, over the phone, I was told that she had left him, but only for a brief time. Apparently, the concern of a stranger, namely me, helped her to realize that she was a human being after all, with rights. So she left him to stew in his own juices for a few weeks. When he asked her to return she told him that she did still love him, but she wanted him the way he was before the children left home. And that she wanted them to spend more time together. And she was ready for a holiday and only when he had booked that holiday would she return. He must have given in, because she was back with him, and although the marriage is still a little rocky, it's not the hell it was. So a happy ending after all.

There's a moral to this story, as my mum used to say. Behave like a doormat, and you'll be treated like one!

19   Jumping Beans

By now you must be thinking that all the clairvoyant visions I tune into are either depressing or frightening. This is certainly not so. My psychic power appears to have developed its own peculiar sense of humour, often presenting me with funny, unusual, embarrassing, or even downright misleading visions. One of the more unusual and funny premonitions happened in the spring of 1985.

I had been invited to a beautiful bungalow in the village of Calverton. I was to read the cards for about six women. The readings turned out to be run of the mill, which wasn't too surprising as most of them were mature, settled, and had fairly happy lives. They had all enjoyed the gathering that evening, even if it had proved to be more amusing than useful. The hostess was the only client who had what I would call a confused reading. She was a tall, slim, fair-haired, attractive woman, with many hobbies from collecting beautiful antique dolls to horse-riding, skiing, squash and swimming. Since divorcing her husband over seven years previously, she had succeeded in a well-paid profession and was totally responsible for her only child, a daughter.

There was a future marriage for her, although she was in no hurry. She enjoyed her life and valued her independence. As I stepped into her future, the only problem I could see involved her daughter, Sharon, who was now almost sixteen. When I predicted that her daughter would need medical attention soon, I was asked to expand on this particular subject. I could see she was eager to tell me about Sharon's health, so I quickly advised her that it was best if she kept any relevant information to herself, for the moment at least.

I find it easier to see and help if I know little, or better still, nothing, about my client and what they believe to be the problem. This way I am not led by the client or how he or she feels. I prefer to depend entirely on my own psychic powers as they don't very often lead me in the wrong direction, whereas a client, without knowing, can send me down many blind alleys.

I settled comfortably into the chair, then cleared my mind ready to accept any relevant vision that would help me to understand, and, with a little luck, solve the problem. The information was readily and freely available for me. It was like switching on a miniature TV inside my head. Crystal clear images depicted Sharon in hospital on an operating table. Two doctors stood by her, scratching their heads, confused by the results, or as it happens, lack of results. On the wall was a great list of unnecessary tests they had done, yet still there was no conclusion. The pictures adopted a cartoon-type quality. One doctor appeared to float around the table. He threw the outrageously large medical book he had been holding at the wall. Then he and the book simply vanished. The second doctor repeated the floating performance. He looked much more menacing because he was waving a surgeon's steel scalpel. The man with the knife never managed to touch Sharon, for suddenly, just like a Walt Disney cartoon, thousands of little jumping beans appeared from within her body. They all had tiny faces, legs and arms. All seemed to have a character of their own, laughing, giggling and scrambling over her and the table. The beans continued to emerge from the child's body, until the operating table was full to overflowing. Then, as they rolled off, the doctor with the knife was inundated by them. He finally disappeared beneath them, never to be seen again. All the funny little beans now started to vanish, waving merrily as they went. The child opened her eyes and smiled. She then rose from the white, sterile operating table and danced through the door. Neither doctor had touched her.

A strange vision indeed, and it took courage to relate this cartoon-type picture to my client, but I did. When I had finished telling her, she gently took me by the arm and silently led me to a small bedroom, Sharon's bedroom. There, on the walls, were hundreds of cartoon characters. Most of them *beans*, although there were a splattering of spaghetti dogs and noodle cats too. This girl had talent that even Walt Disney would have been proud of! I stood and marvelled at the pictures, and realized that this explained why I had received a cartoon-type premonition. However, it did not explain all that I had seen within that psychic vision, and it didn't help with the health problem. So now, much to my disgust, I had to be told the details of Sharon's illness.

Sharon had frequently been ill, over a number of years, with both stomach and head pains. Despite putting her through many tests, doctors had not been able to discover what was causing them. Now they had decided an operation was called for. Sharon was due to attend the hospital in the very near future and to say the least, the child was terrified. I knew I had the answer and it had to be there in the vision. I had to look again, this time with more care. Once again I closed my eyes to the world and concentrated. The now frustrating vision of the beans continued to flash before me. I couldn't get rid of the damn things, they just wouldn't disappear. There had to be another reason, other than Sharon's artistic talent, for them to remain within view. Psychic sense had done all that it could for me. Now it was up to commonsense to work out the cryptic clues within the vision.

'Tell me,' I said, 'does Sharon eat beans as well as draw them? More so than most children?'

Sharon's Mum looked at me quizzically. 'Sharon's crazy about beans. She'd have them for breakfast, dinner and tea if I let her. That's one of the reasons that she draws them. One day when she was little, her dad told her that she'd eventually turn into a bean if she kept eating them at the rate she was doing. The next thing we knew she had created a family of beans. Mummy, Daddy and baby bean, all with the relevant features. From that day on, the drawings just grew like Topsie. It's her favourite pastime. One day she hopes to write children's books all about her bean family.'

There was the answer. Daft as it sounded. Sharon was allergic to *beans*! At least, eating them. Her mum promised to keep her off beans for the next few weeks whilst she was waiting to go into hospital. Although Sharon was reluctant to manage without her favourite food, the temptation of avoiding the hospital appointment and the surgeon's knife was irresistible.

Even as I left the bungalow, both Sharon and her mum were beginning to believe me. What had once been obscure was now quite obvious. After all, no one expects good healthy food like beans to make you ill. Not unless you eat too many, that is!

A few weeks later, a new client told me that she was a friend of Sharon's mum and she had a message for me. Sharon was now well and truly on the road to recovery. The hospital had been able to confirm that it was beans that had been causing the trouble, but only because she had eaten so many of them, far too often. They were just as pleased as Sharon was that operating was no longer necessary, and Sharon could have her beans as long as the portions were small and not too frequent.

20 Delightful Debbi

Diane Blatherwick, a friend of mine and also a psychic investigator, invited me to one of her regular gatherings. This particular meeting was to be held at the local British Legion.

Diane was there to greet my husband and I as we entered the club. Then she led us through to a room where the members of her group were sitting. As I was introduced, one guy went out of his way to impress me. After all, I had just been on TV. This made me a bit of a celebrity, in his eyes anyway. He shook my hand and told me, with great feeling, that even then he could feel my *power*. He said I was strong, very strong, and my vibes were disturbing him. I sincerely hope at this stage you remember what I told you about the fine dividing line between being psychic and psychotic! He deserved an Oscar for his acting, but I've met this type before, so I politely told him that I'd left my broomstick at home along with my psychic powers. This produced the desired effect. He shut up and sat down. I was then introduced to the other members. Most of their names now escape me, but somewhere in that group was Debbi, a cheerful, pretty, absolutely crazy female whom I couldn't help but like. We all sat discussing things that go bump in the night, flying saucers, witchcraft, spooks and spirits, along with the price of drinks, and generally enjoyed ourselves. To people from a distance we must have looked a fairly normal lot, but I felt sorry for those sitting a little closer. It was obvious that we were making them feel uneasy. Nevertheless, the night went well and we all promised to meet up again soon.

I saw Debbi again less than a week later. She wanted a

consultation before I found out too much about her. I had explained at the meeting that the less I knew about a person the better the reading would be. There was also an element of Debbi testing my psychic ability, for the sake of an analytical report to the group at a later date. Whatever the reason for her visit, we found that we got on very well. Her first reading not only turned out to be very accurate, but put me in an unusual, underground situation.

During the reading I told her that she would be moving very soon, much to her delight. Yet the psychic vision of her house was confused. First I saw her in a house, then it changed into a church! Since it's virtually impossible to live in a church, we assumed that she would be living next to one. I went on to say that the house would be expensive and that she would not reside there very long, and advised her to think twice before she moved in. It was then that I decided to take a good long psychic view of the house from the outside. Once again my vision alternated from house to church, which I now ignored. Then I had this strange sensation of being drawn down into the ground. My vision now was that of a mole underground. Even psychically I couldn't stand the claustrophobic conditions. I had to get out. This time it was far easier for me to dismiss my psychic skill and then decipher the cryptic clue above ground, using good old commonsense. The only possible explanation for my subterranean view had to be the sewers. Somewhere, somehow, there had to be a major fault in the system or, in this case, if you will excuse the pun, cistern. I told Debbi to check and double check on the sewers before she moved in as sewer problems are both expensive and messy.

We continued with the reading. I went on to tell her about her forthcoming marriage and the children that she would have. There were lots of other little things that would be of no interest to anyone else, but Debbi was suitably impressed and her report to the members of the psychic club was favourable. Many of her associates became frequent visitors for psychic consultations. Debbi herself was to become a firm friend, often calling for a cup of coffee and a chat. She moved into her house, despite the warning that it would be expensive and have sewer problems, and she adored it. I was invited to see the house as soon as she moved into it. It was the most unusual house that I had ever seen, certainly in tune with Debbi's character. The front of the house was like a church, complete with a vast stained glass window. This started at ground level, spanned the whole of the front of the house, then tapered off to a point at the roof. The inside was on four levels and also unusual. The lounge, which was on top of the kitchen, had a balcony. From here there was the most fantastic panoramic view of Nottingham that I have ever seen. The garden was long and steep, the major part of it wild, with the odd plum and pear tree straining to rise above the weeds and bracken. Debbi, as I said, loved every inch of the garden and the house. She had checked and double checked with the surveyor about the sewers. He was certain that they were in good order, even though he must have thought Debbi wasn't. After all, you have to be a bit crazy if you prefer the advice of a clairvoyant to that of a qualified surveyor! So, she had bought the house and was now happily settling in.

About six months later, I found Debbi, red-faced and fuming, on my doorstep. As I put the kettle on I told her to calm down and tell me what had happened to make her so flustered and angry.

'You and those bloody drains!' she said. 'I've just found out that we are not even connected to the flaming drainage system. Now they tell me that we are connected to a bloody cesspit which, I might add, hasn't been emptied for so long that the sewage is all over the field. We could be prosecuted for not having the damn thing emptied!'

Just watching Debbi marching up and down in my little kitchen, arms waving and swearing like a trooper, was enough to give me a fit of the giggles. It wasn't long before Debbi also saw the funny side of it, despite the seriousness of the situation. Soon we were both laughing as we plotted our course of action.

We found the local council very helpful and everything was settled amicably. Apparently they were partly to blame. When Debbi went home she was much happier and calmer and I was glad to have helped her in this more practical way. I was still right about her not staying there long. Her love of the place was overpowered by her need for adventure. Even as I write these words, Debbi's house is up for sale, and Debbi is looking yet again for another challenge. There is nothing more certain than the fact that she will find it, even if it's on the other side of the world.

21   Believe Kris, Believe

Yes, that's right, sometimes even I can't believe what I see. I try to logically explain psychic vision but it's not always possible. The disbelief in my psychic vision was never stronger than when Grace, a woman in her late thirties, contacted me for psychic assistance.

Grace had married at the tender age of sixteen. The divorce followed less that six years later. She had not conceived during the marriage, although they had tried, but it just wasn't to be. Grace didn't worry about being childless – in fact, she classed it as a blessing in disguise. Once she was free of a jealous husband she had the time, and the opportunity, to start a new career which involved meeting interesting people. As time passed, she came to the conclusion that she was in fact barren, for in all the years of marriage she had never taken any precautions to avoid having children. She quite freely admitted that, in the fifteen years since the divorce, she had had three live-in lovers. Of these, the one she really wanted was married and he had no intention of leaving his wife because she was the one that held the purse-strings. The other two were very pleasant but, when it came to the crunch, they were not quite what she wanted.

Eighteen months ago she met her first husband again at a conference in Birmingham, as they were now both in the same type of business; computers. This was the start of a new romance and they have been seeing each other ever since. Cautiously they moved in together, not really expecting it to work, but as they got to know each other again, they found they were more of a married couple than they ever were in the past.

The reason that Grace now needed psychic advice was

that Paul, her ex-husband and now besotted live-in lover, had asked her to marry him again. She was here to ask me if she *should* marry him again, or would it end in disaster like the last time? This was a vital question for Grace, because she felt that she was too old to make another mistake. As she said, 'It's a lot easier to recover from a broken heart when you're young.'

I looked into the cards for the answer, not that I needed to. My psychic mind had slipped into a search mode without their help – this can and frequently does happen. My clairvoyant senses were telling her to go for it, that this time it would work. She was so pleased to hear this that she almost cried.

That was all she wanted to know. Now she was eager to leave me and get back to Paul. I almost had to physically restrain her.

'Please don't go yet, I haven't finished,' I said.

She returned to her seat, apologetic but still smiling. I gave her time to make herself comfortable. Then I returned to the cards. I didn't like what I was seeing and logically it just didn't appear to be possible, but there it was. As I looked deep into her body I could see the perfect form of a new baby. His heart-beat was strong and fast. I watched him grow as the months raced by, right through to the day he was born. Safe in her arms I now saw her count his ten toes and ten fingers. Her face was the picture of unadultereated bliss. At this moment the sloppy, sentimental side of me also wanted to cry.

Now you tell me, how in hell's name do you tell a woman in her late thirties that she is going to have her first child? Calmly and slowly I said, 'Now you know that your periods have been a bit erratic, don't you?'

The smile was slipping from her face. Now she was curious.

'That's right,' she said. 'I'm in my change, but I'm all right. I'm not suffering like most women do.' She was quite positive.

'Well, I hate to disagree with you, and it's true you are fit, but you should see a doctor.' Now she looked worried, so I had to drop the bombshell quick, before she became too anxious. 'Don't worry, it's nothing serious.' I tried to make light of the situation. 'You're just going to have a baby, millions of women do, you know, every day.'

My effort at being amusing was failing miserably. She sat there stunned, totally disbelieving her own ears or what I'd said, for the best part of a minute.

'You've got to be joking, it can't be, can it?' She was now beginning to think, obviously remembering unusual movements and feelings that she must have had recently. A woman who is over four months pregnant can usually feel the baby as it moves in the womb. 'I thought I was putting a little weight on, but I'd put that down to the fact that I haven't been able to get to my keep fit classes just lately. I've been working hard to try and catch up with a backlog of work.' She looked at me again, then into space. 'No, you have to be wrong, it's impossible.'

'I'm sorry love,' I said, 'I do make mistakes sometimes, but this time I'm certain. Anyway, don't worry about it too much, just get yourself off to the doctor and find out for sure.' Whilst she was still stunned, I thought it would be a good idea to tell her a little more about her future with the baby. So I carried on talking, although I'm not sure if she was listening. 'You and Paul are going to make great parents, you know. He's going to be over the moon. You're not too old, and the baby will be normal, you'll see, everything will be just fine.'

Grace left in a bit of a daze, but promised to make that appointment with the doctor.

It was a good six weeks later when she phoned to confirm my prediction or in this case, diagnosis. She had been in hospital for a few tests to see if the baby was healthy. As far as they could tell, he was one hundred per cent and so was she. Grace said there were hysterics at the clinic when she told the doctors that Kris Sky, clairvoyant, had confirmed the pregnancy. They stopped laughing when they too had to admit that she was pregnant.

Grace came to see me once more, very pregnant, happy and married. The doctors were pleased with her progress and both she and her husband were looking forward to the birth. I told her to keep following the advice of the doctors and she would produce a beautiful baby boy. As for age, well, some people are born old while others are still young when they're ninety. This couple were healthy and very young at heart. I knew that their child would grow up in the right environment with plenty of love.

I haven't seen Grace since then, although they did invite me to the christening. Still, what does she need a clairvoyant for now? She has all she wants, and I was so pleased to be given the honour of announcing a pregnancy before the doctors!

22   The Cry of an Unborn Child

There are quite a few cases where nothing that I say or do will make a blind bit of difference. This type of reading will often upset me for days, until I'm told that the client is over the worst. One young person who succeeded in giving me more than the average amount of restless nights approached me for a consultation recently.

She was a slim bubbly girl, with masses of long red curly hair. This hung in fine ringlets, hiding most of her delicate, pale face. Then it cascaded over her small, somewhat rounded shoulders. Most of her reading was normal to the point of being boring. She had just fallen out with her long-term boyfriend, and, as you could expect, was depressed. Her face started to look a little less tense when I revealed that she would eventually find Mr Right and produce the proverbial 2.3 kids. (Have you ever met anybody that has produced 2.3 kids? No, neither have I! But that's what the national average used to be.) The reading – past, present and future – seemed to fit, and she was over the moon when I told her she would live in Canada. This fact gave the reading a certain amount of credibility, especially since half of her family had been residents there for about ten years. I scanned the cards, just to make sure that I had not missed anything. My eyes were drawn to the section that dealt with health. The voice in my ear screamed at me to look gain, only this time with more care. I then realized that the reading had been so easy that I'd either become sloppy or I was about to find something that I really didn't want to see, feel, or sense. I asked her to bear with me, as I had found some sort of problem, but as of yet, I wasn't sure what it was. She was quite prepared to stay there all day if it was necessary. I made myself more comfortable in the chair. Then I began a mental exercise that I often practise in order to neutralize any physical aggravation around me, like dogs barking, doors banging or even the minor irritation of the clock ticking. This exercise requires me to mentally visualize all my muscles relaxing and tensing two or three times. As soon as my body is completely at ease, the psychic side of my brain slowly drifts deeper and deeper into a great dark chasm. This frequently leads me into the future, or as it was for this client, reveals the unknown medical problems of today. I'm quite familiar with this maze, and as a rule I find myself in pitch black darkness. Then as I continue to walk, a pin-point of light invariably intensifies, until I'm able to see all that appears before me. It's in these illuminated areas that I can usually see into the future or find the answers to my questions. On this occasion there was no bright revealing light, just a thick pea soup-type fog that felt wet as it swirled around me. Then I had the strange sensation of shrinking to the size of a small rabbit. My brain was still wrestling with this predicament, when it was literally tied up with another. The whole of my body became conscious of being bound with invisible and life extinguishing wires. My heart-beat raced uncontrollably, and the blood pulsating around my head made me physically sick. I could stand the sensation no longer; it was too depressing. Releasing the vision activated the methodical part of my mind, which brought me back to the present situation. Once again I had the awe-inspiring job of telling a young woman that she was pregnant. Only this time there would be no happy ending. When I told her, she was abrupt to the point of being offensive, accusing me of scaremongering. Then she went on to tell me that there was no way she could be pregnant. With this she got up to go. Reluctantly she opened her purse, saying that I really wasn't worthy paying, but she would anyway. I refused her money and told her to pay me later if she wanted to, but in the meantime, it was vital that she visited a doctor.

She left the house in a huff, forgetting that all I had told her about the past had been correct. Because she was still so broken-hearted over the last boyfriend, mentally she'd refused to accept that there could still be any connection between them. A baby was the last thing she wanted as a momento.

I did worry about her. Every so often I would find myself thinking about the experience that I had had during her reading. Then I wondered if I was letting this psychic thing get to me. Perhaps this was one time when I had let psychic sense present me with a misleading little melodrama, which I had foolishly believed. Question after question rolled around my head until some nights I was dizzy. Only when the client's mother phoned was I put out of my misery and allowed to get a full night's sleep.

Apparently, the young woman was rushed into hospital less than a week later. She had suddenly come down with crippling stomach pains and her mother had phoned for the ambulance. The girl had conceived despite being fitted with the coil. Obviously she was very upset, because there was no possibility of saving the baby. Then, once she was over the initial shock, she had told her mum that she knew she would be all right because she had remembered me saying so. Now all she had to do was get well, ready for Mr Right and her future children.

Now that I knew the client was safe, I found I was free to analyze the visions and sensations this reading had brought about. I firmly believe that the wet grey fog I first encountered within the vision must have been the fluid that surrounds a baby whilst it is in the womb. The invisible wires could have been the coil that had twisted around the child, eventually depriving it of life. I, for the very briefest moment, had entered that same baby's mind and suffered as he or she had. Sad, so very sad, but inevitable. One wonders if, one day, we will find out why any innocent little child should ever suffer, albeit unintentionally, on our behalf.

23   Gaining Stones Loses Pounds

I find that babies frequently feature within my consultations. Some women want them and can't have them.
Others have them and don't want them. I suppose I must
be lucky, because I know both feelings, all too well!

I found this account about women and babies funny,
interesting and different. More than that however, there's
a valuable lesson to be learnt here. Even the most talented
and experienced psychic in the world has not got one
hundred per cent vision. Often I'm only given a small
piece of a jigsaw puzzle. The remaining parts of the puzzle
are scattered somewhere in the future, and only the
passage of time will reveal the full picture.

Approximately two years ago I was invited to a party
booking, somewhere in West Bridgford. This is a wealthy
residential area and I was a bit skitty (my word for being
nervous) about meeting these people. I needn't have
worried – the hostess had inherited the house and now
she and her husband were struggling to adapt it to their
style of life. They were both very pleasant, hard-working
people. He was a policeman and she was the secretary to a
group of local doctors.

The women that night varied in age and background
and even the occasional male ventured through to see me.
This usually happens when the wife tells the husband that
I've been able to reveal some very personal fact. Curiosity
eventually gets the better of him, then just for a laugh, you
understand, a very sceptic male will honour me with his
presence for a reading. Men have a different attitude to
women with regard to clairvoyance. So, later on in the
book you will find that I have dedicated a whole chapter to

reading for men. But this particular story is about the hostess.

The hostess, on this occasion, was the last person to come through for a consultation. Her spotlessly clean kitchen had become my reading room for the night. She had been very thoughtful, sending me a glass of wine through with almost every client. Most of the wine, much to my disgust, went down a very convenient sink. Since I'm more of a lager drinker. I have to admit that by this time I was a little tipsy. I had avoided most of the drinks, but now here she was, glass in hand, insisting that I must be thirsty because I had been talking for so long. Feeling that it would have been discourteous to refuse, I smiled sweetly, thanked her, then secretly prayed that this last reading was going to be quick and easy. My prayers were ignored, as usual. This consultation was to be a real brain rattler.

The hostess (we'll call her Julie) was a pretty, blonde woman. She was only five feet tall, but about two stone overweight. We all know that a couple of stones over the top is not an awful lot if you're lucky enough to be six feet tall. There's room for the fat to spread out more evenly! However, when you're small, the problem becomes much more obvious. The weight wasn't Julie's major concern though, for she had been married for over six years and desperately wanted a child. I immediately told her that there was no reason for her to worry. I could see not only one child in the future, but four of them. Talk about one extreme to the other! All that was wrong was their timing. He had been working overtime for ages, due to the fact that this was the year the miners had been on strike. Soon, the strike and his overtime would come to an end. Mother nature would then take over, and bingo, four kids in six years.

She was really pleased with her reading and I don't think it would have bothered her if I'd said there were a dozen kids in the future. For her it was a case of the more the merrier.

Just as she was about to leave the table she rather coyly said, almost as if she thought she was asking for too much, 'Do you think that you could help me with another little problem?' My prayers were not only being ignored, but someone up there was making me pay penance for having the audacity to ask in the first place. She continued. 'I know this may sound silly but as you can see, I have to lose some weight. I've tried all the diets going but I always fall by the wayside after about two weeks.'

She looked so lost, I had to help her. I asked her to sit down again.

'Well love,' I said, 'I'll try, but don't hold your breath. I'm a clairvoyant not a dietician.'

With that, I prepared to enter the mental maze containing most, and I do emphasize the word *most*, of the answers to my questions. I found the way deeper and darker than usual. This could have been because this was not a life or death situation. My psychic senses were making me work extra hard to find the solution to what may have been a petty or vain problem. It was almost as if I had no right to agitate it into action purely for the sake of some poor woman's vanity. But this time I was determined to win – either that or the booze was making me stubborn. Anyway I stuck with it, refusing to leave the great black hole I was in until I was given some sort of answer.

The light began to shine at the end of the tunnel as I walked closer and closer. Then, before me appeared a small round porthole type window. I was not going to be allowed to go any further. It was from this position that I would have to watch my client. As soon as the vision became clear, I saw Julie step from the kitchen, then walk down her garden. She appeared to stoop and pick up something small, but I couldn't see what it was. The view became cloudy and dark, then just as if it was on a video and had been rewound, it was presented to me once again.

This time my position, along with that of the porthole, had been relocated to the area in the garden where Julie had bent down. Now as I watched, I could see exactly what Julie had picked up. Not that it made much sense. Julie had gone down the garden and picked up a small stone, then she discarded that one and proceeded to select another. This one seemed much more satisfactory. She then returned to her kitchen, stone or pebble in hand, and through the window, I watched as she examined it. The clouds reappeared, then the whole process was repeated, again and again. The only thing that did change was Julie's size. She was becoming slimmer and slimmer as each vision was replayed.

As I warned you at the beginning of this story, the whole picture is not always presented to me. I hadn't got all the answers, or even what I would have considered half an answer. This was one case where it would be necessary to wait for time to put the last pieces of the puzzle into place.

'Look,' I said to Julie, 'I know this sounds daft, but the only way that you are going to lose weight is by going into the garden, and picking up a stone. I know, it sounds crazy to me as well, but that's what I saw. You going down the garden, selecting stones and pebbles, then you appeared to get slimmer. I'm afraid it's a very cryptic clue to your weight loss. However, you've got nowt to lose but weight if you try it.'

We both laughed, then decided that we'd had too much to drink. She thanked me for trying anyway, and said that she and all her friends had had a smashing night. She said she would definitely be inviting me back in the New Year. With that, a slightly tiddly clairvoyant went home. In a taxi, I hasten to add.

Eighteen months later, I did arrive back at the same house. I didn't recognize the lady who greeted me with a great big smile. As you know, I do have this cullender-type memory that has the habit of retaining only the most useless type of information! I was quickly led into the kitchen, where I started to recall my previous visit. However, the kitchen had gone through an astonishing change. All around the room were little animals and birds made of stones and shells. They were all beautifully varnished and painted, but they were everywhere. On the fridge, the cooker, the window-sill, across the side units and even on the floor. One particularly large stone, now looking distinctly like an arrogant fat frog, had been used as a door stop. If there was space for another pebble, I couldn't have found it! I turned to see the hostess smiling back at me – obviously she thought I'd remembered her last reading, but I hadn't.

'See,' she said, 'it worked.' She then pirouetted in the doorway of the kitchen, showing off her slim figure. Then and only then did the penny drop. Good grief, now I recognized her. She was the hostess from over a year ago. I was still a little confused, so she had to explain to me exactly how her last reading had helped her to lose so much weight, so fast. After all, I could do with losing a few extra pounds myself, and if it worked for her there was still hope for me. Apparently she had done just as I had said. The day after her first consultation with me, maybe because she was a little depressed, she had gone down the garden as she had in my vision. Whilst she was there, she had set eyes on a stone that looked like a tiny mouse. So she had taken it into the kitchen, painted it, put a tail on it, then given it to her three-year-old nephew to play with. He loved it but said it was lonely, so she had to find it the ideal 'stone mate' the next day. Soon there was a complete family, and my client had a new hobby. The hobby quickly developed into a business and her once-hidden talent was now making her a small amount of money. The spin-off was that whilst she was making her stone animals and earning money, she wasn't tucking into the fridge, so naturally she was losing weight. Not that it would last very long. Soon that trim, slim figure would have to support a growing baby and this would complete her happiness.

24   Lovely Legs Prevent Pain

Twenty years ago it was very rare that I had the opportunity to read for a man, young or old, but this is not so these days. There has been a change in the proportion of men to women who seek psychic assistance, and now approximately forty per cent of my clientele are male.

The men who dare to enter what was once considered a predominantly female domain are usually successful, intelligent and open-minded. Yet they still display a certain amount of scepticism. This frequently gives me a chance to, shall we say, show off. Why? you may ask. Well, I'll tell you. It's far easier to impress a person who doubts psychic power, than it is to impress someone who knows exactly what this power is capable of.

Men are only just beginning to understand the full potential of psychic power. This is partly because there are now enough machines, computers and experts able to scientifically test the psychic capabilities of the brain – that which is often referred to as the sixth sense. These machines and experts will often provide enough clinical data to sway even the most bigoted disbeliever. Men are now beginning to believe what most women have always known. Psychic power in its many forms not only exists, but it works!

Now let me tell you about Ian, a young man who was still sitting on the fence, as my mum would have put it. He had psychic power, but he didn't want to believe it. It didn't go with the macho image he was trying to portray. Recently his ability to see into the future had frightened him, and at the same time, kept him alive. For no apparent reason, he'd refused to get into a car which one of his mates was driving. After making some daft excuse, he told them that he would be walking home, so they left him. The car was involved in a fatal accident, and Ian lost two good mates that night. He now felt guilty that he had not stopped his friends driving away. And he still didn't know what made him refuse to get into the car in the first place.

Eventually, he had found the courage to come for a reading. Somewhere at the back of his mind, he knew that there had to be something in it, 'it' being psychic ability. But he still needed facts, preferably something on paper in black and white. He hoped I was going to be the one to prove to him that psychic ability really does exist and that he wasn't on his way to the madhouse. The other reason for his visit was to find out why he hadn't stopped his friends from driving to their deaths. I told Ian that even I have difficulty in explaining my psychic feelings, thoughts or visions. Often it's impossible to know just what the sixth sense is trying to transmit to you. It's a bit like catching smoke. You put your hand out and know you've grasped it, but then, a fraction of a second later, it's gone. If I'd been in Ian's place I would have probably done exactly the same thing, even with my psychic training. Ian started to relax. Knowing that an experienced psychic would have done precisely as he had lifted an awful lot of weight and guilt from his shoulders. Now it was time to prove that my clairvoyant talent was as good as my counselling and listening abilities. A good reading was vital if I was to consolidate the guilt-erasing advice I had just given to him. Free from anxiety, Ian's face adopted a rather cheeky smile that instantly made him look younger than I'd originally thought. He shuffled the cards and I began the reading. I started as usual, with his personality, and the thoughts that he had been toying with for some time. I told him, without hesitation, that one of his dreams was to visit Canada. Then I revealed that he could have gone the previous year if he hadn't got involved with a highly unsuitable and expensive female. This was spot on and I was only just beginning to show off! He had to agree with me when I said that he had strong paternal instincts. If it was up to him, his future wife would have to produce a football team, and that would be just to start with, poor girl.

When examining his home life, I came across not one, but two mothers. This confused me and I couldn't decide whether he'd been adopted or not. His biological mother was certainly still alive although he appeared to reside with another woman. It was this woman whom he loved and related to as a mum. This really rattled him. He actually lived with his gran and had done for years. He loved his mum, but they were always arguing. He got on much better with his beloved gran. Now he was truly beginning to believe in psychic power. The trouble was, he was over the top. Anything I said now would be taken as gospel, and that's the last thing I ever want. As I tell all my clients, no psychic has one hundred per cent vision. We are only allowed small glimpses into the future, and these can often be cloudy. It's not that I didn't want him to believe in psychic power – after all, it's my job to prove exactly what psychic power is capable of – but it was all important that he understood its limitations as well.

We continued with the reading, talking about his career and ambitions, then I went into his health. He was a very fit young man. He had the correct amount of respect for his body; neither abusing nor worshipping it. I expected him to live a long and healthy life.

As I tried to leave this section and go into the set that dealt with wealth, I felt a burning sensation race across my face. For a moment I thought I must have been blushing, but the pain became more intense. As I sat there I could not only feel the pain, but my arm actually started to go red. This client was due to suffer the searing pain that is usually associated with that of a burn or scold. His face and arm would be severely affected unless I could do something about it. Have you ever had one of those conversations with yourself whereby you go round and round in circles? Then, after exploring every facet, you still end up with a stupid answer. Well this was the type of conversation I was having. Kris, I told myself, make up your bloody mind. First, you go out of your way to prove to him that psychic power does exist, so that he doesn't think he's going crazy. Then you tell him it's not that good, because you don't want him to feel guilty about his mates dying. Then you show off, which only succeeded in taking him over the top. Then, clever clogs, you had to slap him down and warn him that psychic power has its limitations. Now you want him to believe every flaming word you say because you don't want him to get hurt! It's no wonder he's confused, because you are too. This conversation was getting out of hand. I was losing, would you believe? I had to decide what was most important. Ian's belief or disbelief now held second place. I was determined he wasn't going to suffer that burn. So, if it meant he would have to leave me with a slightly distorted view of psychic power, so be it and to hell with the consequences. I told him exactly what I'd been feeling. I didn't want to frighten him, but if we were going to avoid this unnecessary incident he had to have all the facts I could give him. He realized how serious I was when he too saw my arm, which by now was very red and inflamed. I then asked him to give me a few moments so that I could prepare myself to enter my black hole. I know that this is only a symbolic chamber but believe me, when you're about to see something you know is not going to be very pleasant, the task is not easily entered into. Especially since I'm a bit squeamish. I'd never have made a nurse.

I visualized the entrance to the tunnel, then I walked through into the depths of the blackest shadows, certain that I would soon be allowed a glimpse into this young man's future. The darkness wrapped itself around me, then quickly cleared. I found myself squinting against brilliant sunshine. My eyes took a few moments to adjust to the sunlight. Then, all too clearly, a vision was set before me. Two of the most attractive female legs I have ever seen anywhere were displayed to perfection. Whoever she was, she could have made a fortune modelling tights or stockings. I barely had time to envy her when an excruciating pain shot across my arm and face, leaving me no alternative but to return to the present. I had no choice. I was back with my client and as such, had no real explanation to help him. This was desperately disappointing for me as it is always very important to get as much detail as I can for my client's benefit.

However, the pure pain of this vision would not allow me to stay with it. So I just had to tell Ian all that I'd seen, and hope that it would be enough to stop him getting seriously burnt. How he laughed when I told him that the only thing that would save him from being badly burnt was the vision of a pair of very lovely legs. He was still laughing when he left and I can't say I blamed him. I was sure that he had not heeded my warning. In this, I am glad to say, I was proved wrong.

Ian contacted me less than a week later. The previous day, as he was travelling back from the coast, he'd spotted two young damsels in distress. They were having problems with their car, and since it was in Ian's nature to play sir Galahad, he'd stopped to help them. (The girls were very attractive so this made his task much more enjoyable!) Their car had overheated and they were waiting for it to cool down. Our knight of the road went to his car to fetch an old sack and the water he always carried. He then dropped the sack over the radiator so that he wouldn't burn his hand. Wise man, I thought. He then told me that at that moment his reading with me was the furthest thing from his mind. It was pure commonsense that made him put the sack over the hot radiator. It was as he was leaning on the bonnet of the car that, from the corner of his eye, he could see one of the bored girls now leaning on a fence. She was wearing the very shortest shorts he'd ever seen. In order to, shall we say, improve his view, he had to lean further and further over the bonnet of the car. It was as the view became almost irresistible that it happened. He said that he heard me shout 'LEGS!' and then at the same time he had the strangest sensation that I was actually pulling him back. At that very second the radiator exploded, spraying red-hot water everywhere, startling them all. All Ian had suffered was a slight burn to his hand, but that was painful enough. His face and arms were free from burns and pain. The girls said he was lucky to escape with such minor burns, and he had to agree. However, he said it was the vision of the girl's legs and the sound of my voice which had prevented him from being scarred for life. Never, ever again would he laugh at me or my predictions.

25 Confused Clairvoyant

My readings from time to time can be, to say the least, confused and distorted. This type of situation can frequently bring about a fit of the giggles from either my client or myself. Such was the case of John Grant.

He arrived for his reading wearing a blue short-sleeved summer shirt, absolutely wet through to the skin. Apparently it had been fine when he had started his journey, but our infamous British weather had only lulled him into a false sense of security. As soon as he was halfway between his home and my office, down came the rain. He gratefully accepted the towel that I gave him, but shyly declined my offer to dry his shirt. I waited for him to dry himself as best as he could, then tried to start his reading. I say tried, because we were both still laughing about his dilemma. He sat there, his hair messed up from being towel-dried and his shirt sticking to his chest. His happy smiling face reminded me of a man who could always make me laugh – Norman Wisdom.

I started his reading as I always do, analyzing his personality. John was a clever, adaptable, artistic and thoughtful man. He had been married, but that hadn't lasted long, so he must have had some faults, but either I couldn't reveal them, or I didn't want to see. He had lived alone for the past seven years in an old house that he had enjoyed restoring to its original, though somewhat ornate, condition. This had taken a lot of time, hard work, money and patience, which was why I was totally unprepared for the forthcoming psychic view of him.

There he stood, in my clairvoyant vision, throwing beautiful crockery at the wall. I couldn't believe what I was seeing. I had just analyzed this man's character and he certainly wasn't the type to willingly destroy anything, so I decided to keep this vision to myself. It was too much out of character for me to believe. The next vision I had was much more to my liking. First of all I saw him take up a large paintbrush, then he started to paint the wall. He agreed that he had been doing quite a lot of painting just lately. Then the scene changed, ever so slightly. The brush in his hand shrank to the size of an artist's brush. The image that now slowly developed in front of him was of a glorious white horse. Two seconds later, the horse had sprouted large, angelic wings. This was the most fantastic, lifelike portrait I had ever seen of Pegasus, the winged steed of the Greek gods. John was amazed, saying that he'd just finished such a painting, but he had been disappointed with the final result. When I explained how I had seen the picture, he said that he too had the same mental picture, but it just didn't come to life on canvas. Maybe I was picking up what he had wanted to paint, not what was actually there – I would have loved to have seen his painting. This man had set himself a very high standard.

We continued with the reading. I don't recall much more about it, but we did still find quite a few things to laugh about. The session was about to finish but, being a curious cat, I still found time to venture once again into the first vision that I had had of John. It wasn't difficult to find, logged in the back of my brain like some sort of computerized fact on a floppy disc, readily available for me if and when I should require it. I watched as this gentle man destroyed vases, cups and plates by throwing them viciously at a wall. I was bewildered; mortified even. I certainly wasn't going to let John go until I had solved the mystery, or I'd never sleep.

'Why,' I said, obviously perplexed, 'why do I see you smashing pots by the dozen?' He now looked as confused as I felt. I continued. 'That's the view of you that I keep getting. I don't know, maybe you're fed up with the pots you've got. Perhaps you're just ready for a change, but I'm telling you, there's a much easier way of getting rid of unwanted pots. You could just as easily give them away. Then you wouldn't have the hassle of cleaning them up once you've thrown them at the wall.'

Something must have clicked. For the next ten minutes John was reduced by uncontrollable laughter to a gibbering idiot, unable to string two words together. I found his Norman Wisdom face and incapability to talk slightly amusing, but I was still in the dark as to what had brought about this hysterical moment, and this annoyed me. Once he had regained some composure, he told me, between giggles, that his hobby was in fact, pot throwing. His mother had taught him the craft many years ago and after her death he had inherited her potter's wheel and kiln. When the world was against him or he felt sad and lonely he would take up the clay and start moulding. The very act of spinning relieved him of all anxiety, but more importantly, made him feel closer to his mother. However, he assured me that the wet clay usually hit the potter's wheel and not the wall!

26 A Miner with a Major Problem

It isn't always women who find themselves in a predicament they can't see any way out of. Sometimes, even a man with the physical and mental strength to work in the mines will suddenly sink into the depths of depression, entombing him in misery, darkness and despair.

Robert was such a man. He came to me, as most people do, when all else had failed. His face was dark, not only with coal-dust. For no matter how much a miner washes, he never succeeds in removing the black mascara-type dust from his eyes. Or the blue-black scars from his skin. No, this man's face was stained with utter despair. Miners don't cry, or so I've been led to believe, and this man certainly wasn't going to in my presence. But the tears were there, deep inside him, along with the heartbreak and pain that now ate away at his guts.

His wife, a woman that he worshipped, had found another man. Now she wanted to be free of a marriage that had been on the rocks for ages. Robert knew that she hadn't been happy. He had tried to give her everything that she'd asked for, but it just wasn't enough. Two months ago, he'd come home from work to find that she had packed her bags and gone, leaving him and the children so that she could be with her new lover. My client still loved her – it didn't matter what she had done – nothing could destroy his love for her. This gentle, kind man did not know how to cope with his own heartache, let alone have the courage to explain and comfort his children. The days and long lonely nights passed into weeks and then months. Still he waited for her to return. Only the love and devotion of his children stopped him from committing suicide. I wanted to tell him she'd be back, for this was what he was longing to hear. At that time it would have been all too easy to put this poor man out of his misery – for a few weeks anyway. I wanted to paint for him the prettiest, happiest picture of the future that you could ever imagine. I sat there, trapped between the desire to ease his torment, and my own moral code of ethics which denied me the luxury of lying.

Suddenly, Psy, the mystery man from my dream desert, my psychic guardian no less, sent out a high-pitched, brain-scrambling, whistle, which was both painful and disorientating. Psy must have realized that I needed his help with this case. Or maybe he just didn't trust me, knowing I have a soft spot for miners. Whatever the reason for his unexpected daytime visit, I was still pleased to sense him around me. The reading now had to be a good one. With Psy there beside me I couldn't go wrong. This consultation was one of the best I've ever done.

First and foremost Robert had to know that although his wife would come back, it would be for all the wrong reasons, and she wouldn't be staying for long. This was a little like giving a child sweets, then grabbing them back because they'd rot his teeth or make him sick. But that's what his wife was, a slow poison. A poison which would eventually kill him if he didn't find the antidote soon. Knowing that she would return gave him the will to live. The fact that she wouldn't be staying gave him the time to prepare to survive, eventually without her.

Psy, my invisible visitor, whispered in my ear, this time with a little more consideration for me. He was now encouraging me to go on with the reading, telling me that I was capable of improving this man's life almost beyond recognition. Robert was totally unaware of the many qualities within him. To start with I told him he was a natural writer and comedian. This came as more of a surprise to him that it did to me, but it was important that he knew. You see, he'd never attempted to do anything different to what the rest of his family had done. His dad had been a miner and so had his grandad; even his brothers worked down the mines. Miners, proud of their reputations for being tough, don't usually dabble with anything that stinks of being effeminate or 'cissy'. I encouraged Robert to try to put pen to paper – after all, no one had to know what he was doing in the privacy of his own home. The next step he would have to take, if he was going to discover half that he was capable of, was to be much more difficult. I cautiously advised him to find the local repertory theatre and join the damn thing. There he would meet people from all walks of life who would give him the courage to break away from the restricting routine lifestyle he'd been leading. Robert was more than a little sceptical about this part of his reading, but at least he listened. We went on to talk about his children and work, then religion and love. He was relieved to know that he would always have his children, and that they would not suffer too much because their mum had left them. I went on to tell him that a very special person would soon enter his life, someone who would help him to put his life into some sort of order. Although she was not a future wife, there would be a friendship between them they would both value in the years to come. As Robert left, he was honest enough to tell me that he had his doubts about an awful lot of my predictions. Some, he said, went completely against the grain. However, he also said that just talking to me had made him feel better. Somehow the clouds around him were not quite as depressing and black now. I believe that Psy had spun a healing web around Robert, just to help him get through the next few days. Ultimately though, Robert would be responsible for his own welfare. He only needed help with the first few steps, then he would start a new and much more interesting life. Not long after his first consultation, I received a lovely letter from Robert, thanking me for the peace and tranquility he had found on the night of the reading. I silently passed his thanks on to Psy because I think he had more to do with Robert getting a good night's sleep than I did. Even as I read the letter, I could see that he certainly had a way with words for someone who rarely put pen to paper. I saw him again, about six months later, when he brought one of his new-found friends along with him for a reading. She turned out to be the special lady I had told him about. He also told me that he had started to write, and actually entered a minor competition for new authors. He didn't expect to win, but he was really chuffed that he had managed to complete a small but interesting manuscript.

One of his children had joined a local theatre group and had literally dragged him along. This had resulted in him helping with the scenery, and as I said, finding many new friends. It no longer mattered what the rest of his family thought; he was enjoying himself. His children had survived the trauma of being separated from their mother. They had always loved their dad, but now he was much more fun to be with and the kids were making the most of it. I knew they would all benefit from this new adventurous dad who loved them so much. As for his wife, well, she did return, but this time he was prepared for her. He told her straight. He'd have her back this time, but this was going to be the very last time. Her coming and going as she pleased was too upsetting for him and the kids so he had to draw the line, no matter how much he loved her. She stayed one night, but returned to her lover the next day. Robert was still very upset, but he said that laying down the law that one night made him feel just a little bit better about himself. Somewhere in the last conversation with his now ex-wife, he'd found the dignity and pride that had been missing from his life for so long.

Robert's Letter

Dear Kris,

I am the man that you did the emergency reading for on Monday last. I am writing to thank you once again for the tremendous help you gave me. I left your house with a feeling of peace, the like which I haven't felt for a very long time. It stayed with me until I went to bed, where I slept a sound refreshing sleep.

Today I must admit, I've been in tears for some moments, but through it all, something, not exactly a voice, seems to be saying to me, 'Let things unfold, we'll take care of you.' I also feel that I am about to regain control of my life again. The old maxim, 'Life's for learning', has suddenly taken on a very special and personal meaning for me. Regarding the book that you are engaged in writing. This may sound a little vain, believe me it's not intended to, but you have my full permission to refer to my 'case' should you so wish, but then again I am sure that you have encountered much more memorable people than myself.

Once again, sincere thanks to you, I'll never forget meeting you, may you enjoy continuous harmony and peace, qualities the germination of which you helped to implant in my soul.

May we meet again.

Robert.

27 Ladies of the Night

As a practising clairvoyant, I get to see many people from all walks of life. My clientele spans a vast range of professions, from barristers to teachers, doctors to dentists, steeplejacks to miners. Most of my clients benefit and, I hope, learn a little from their consultations. I, on the other hand, am often intrigued and fascinated by their lifestyles. This was never more true than the evening I met the 'ladies of the night'. This particularly dark winter's night, my husband and I ventured out to a booking at the infamous Hyson Green in Nottingham. Try as we may, the address seemed to elude us. John stopped the car to ask directions and the only person in sight was a young woman perched on a road sign. She may or may not have had a skirt on; it was difficult to tell as a three-quarter coat covered all she had on, and this was the shortest three-quarter coat that I'd ever seen. Her black stockings and high-heeled shoes displayed her legs to perfection. She wore far too much make-up, which she didn't need to make her look attractive. No, the heavy make-up was like a badge to let you know she was a prostitute and ready for business.

'Go and ask her if she knows where this particular walk is,' John said. I didn't like the idea of approaching her, so I looked all about me. My luck wasn't in, there was no one else about. The streets were empty.

'You go and ask her,' I said, 'you know I'm no good at taking directions.'

John looked at me with complete disbelief, then said, 'Don't be bloody stupid, woman. If I go out there, she could think I was a customer. Or worse still, what if a copper sees me and thinks I'm trying to pick her up. I could get done, you daft bat!'

He sat there, safe behind his steering wheel. There was no way he was going to move. So if I was going to get to this booking, I was the one who had to get the directions.

The girl was quite pleasant and told me the reason we couldn't find the address was because we weren't looking high enough. The walk that I needed was in the great housing complex behind us. This rose in many sections to six storeys high. There were even streets, way up high in the sky above me. I thanked her, then went back to the car with the relevant information. I told John to park the car, as the only way to get to this address was on foot, and I wasn't going to go alone.

We both trudged up two flights of stairs, across one of the streets in the sky, then up another flight of steps that put us on some sort of alley. We picked our way past dogs and dustbins, avoiding the sinister-looking people as best we could. By this time all I wanted to do was go home. If I'd have known I was coming to an area like this, I wouldn't have taken the booking in the first place. Too late, a door opened almost as we passed it and a strange voice said, 'Hey there, are you Kris Sky?'

'Yes,' I said, relieved to find that the owner of the voice had a friendly face. The light from the doorway made me feel less nervous.

'My name's Clair,' she said, 'I'm the one that booked you for the night. Please come in.'

My husband started to back away, saying that he was going home and I was to phone him when I'd finished. With that he was on his way back to his precious car.

The flat was small and fussy but very clean. There were photos of children all over the walls. Four women were waiting for a reading and Clair told me that there would be two more coming later. The women were much the same as any others; fat, thin, young and old. Just normal women in fact, and even though I knew they were all prostitutes, I began to relax. I was amazed to find that they were kind, funny, considerate and in quite a few cases very clever – not in the least bit as I had been led to believe. I dropped some real clangers that night and my naivety brought about many laughs.

One woman with a broad Scottish accent was intently listening to all that I had to tell her and the mood was very sombre. I told her it was essential that she started to look after herself better and not do too much work or she would end up on her back in bed for months. Well I ask you, what a stupid thing to say. It wasn't until I realized exactly what I had said that I started to blush every shade of red and purple going. Oh, how she laughed at my embarrassment. Her broad Scot accent rolled as she said, 'Well gal, that's the best news I've had for months. Business has been lousy, and now you've got the gall to tell me that I'm gonna to be on me back for months. Do you think it's a sign that business will pick up then?'

I still blush when I think about my stupidity that night. I could still hear her laughter as I read for the next client. Only this reading turned out to be much more serious.

This young girl was only about twenty years old. She already had a little girl of two, to whom she was devoted. She'd left home after she had become pregnant and had not been back since. It was the usual story. She didn't think her mum would want to have anything to do with her and she was certain that her dad would have killed her. So she'd left home and the only way she could earn money was to go on the game. She admitted that she could have worked in a shop, but she needed money fast, to furnish her flat and keep her baby. She had not contacted the D.S.S. because she was afraid they would take her baby from her. Prostitution was her only way out. However, the job which had enabled her to keep her child was now about to deprive her of it. She had been picked up by the police for plying her trade in the streets. She was now waiting to go to court for her third offence. There was nothing more certain than the fact that she would end up in prison. Not that she was afraid of this. No, she was only worried about her child. Now she desperately wanted me to help her in any way I could. Though how in hell's name I was going to help her was, at that moment, beyond me. I spent about three minutes preparing myself to enter that part of my brain which will often reveal to me the problem and then the solution. This view then enables me to see a way round things. Then sometimes, just sometimes, it's possible to make a slight alteration. Clearing and improving the future path for the client. With psychic vision, I saw her in court. She cried as her baby was taken from her, then she was sent down. The vision was then rerun, and there were a few alterations. This time there was an older woman at my client's side. Undoubtedly her mother, and she now held the little one, her grandaughter. Then the vision changed yet again. This time I saw my client visiting a hospital bed. In the bed was a man, tired and looking older than his years. He greeted her with open arms, tears of love and sorrow filling his eyes. He wanted and loved his long lost daughter, no matter what she had become or done. I knew that the only way this young woman was going to avoid prison and keep her child, was to contact her mother. She wasn't keen. It had been a long time since she'd seen her and they weren't that close before. She asked me if I was sure, almost begging me to find another way, but I had to tell her that this was the only way. With that she said that she would at least contact her mum, but she still didn't think it would make any difference. However, she'd have tried anything if it meant she could keep her daughter.

She phoned me a few weeks later to tell me she'd met her mum and they were friends again. Her dad was in hospital; he had some sort of cancer, but it was treatable and there was no fear of him dying in the near future. However, his illness had been a shock to him and made him think about the daughter he hadn't seen for so long, and could have lost for good. He now wanted a second chance with both his daughter and his new-found grandaughter. She still had to go to court, but they were very lenient towards her and let her off with yet another caution. This was on the condition that she stayed with her parents and kept away from her prostitute friends. This, she said, was going to be difficult, but she would comply with the court order. Nothing was more important than her daughter.

With the next client I made the mistake of expressing my belief that all prostitutes are dragged into their profession kicking and screaming by some big fat pimp. This is just not so, and this young attractive woman soon put me in my place when I was daft enough to tell her that she was far too intelligent and pretty to be on the game.

'Look,' she said with a strength and knowledge that was way beyond her years. 'I haven't come here for you to preach at me. If I'd wanted that I could have gone home to my mum. Now, are you going to preach at me or read my cards?'

'Sorry' sounded a bit lame and stupid, but it was all that this addled brain of mine could come up with. So to make up for being so supercilious, I took more care with her reading and made it extra long.

She enjoyed her work and had a very good future in store for her. Eventually she would marry exceptionally well, but it wouldn't be in this country. All the time I was reading for her I felt as if I was flying. Sometimes this only means that the client will take a continental holiday in the near future. But this sensation had a finality about it. A feeling of being at home, and settling in the other country. Then I saw the Statue of Liberty and knew that this young woman was sure to find her fortune in America. As soon as I'd said this, she opened the large expensive handbag resting at her feet. She then produced two air tickets. Destination? Well, you've guessed it – America. All she wanted to know was, had she made the right decision to go to America? She was sad about leaving all her friends and worried that she would not be successful enough to return to England if she wanted to. Now she could leave England and her friends, happy with the knowledge that if she needed to return, she would be both able and wealthy enough to, even if it was only for a holiday.

The rest of the evening went well and I really did enjoy my evening with the 'ladies of the night' from Hyson Green. They taught me not to always believe what I had heard or read. This, for me, was both a memorable and valuable lesson on life!

28   Meeting the Media

Because people are becoming much more curious about psychic ability, I now find that the media, i.e. newspapers, radio and TV, are interested in interviewing me. This gives me the very pleasant opportunity to occasionally mix with the elite (well, a few celebrities anyway).

As soon as I am approached by the media, my knees turn to jelly. My brain goes on holiday and my mouth plays on forty-five when it should be on seventy-eight or vice versa. It would be painful for me to describe the end result caused by these conditions. So, I'll just leave you to have a good laugh as you imagine the overall effect.

Why I suffer so painfully before every interview is a mystery, because I have always found nothing but warm, friendly and considerate people around me. When I went to Central Television studios in Birmingham, I found everyone had a smile and a few minutes chat for me. The girls in make-up were extremely kind and very interested in the subject of clairvoyance. Producers, presenters, researchers and the many technicians employed by Central Television were efficient, helpful and sympathetic. I remember that I had quite a funny experience with one of the sound men. Just before I went on the set, he had to clip a small microphone to the lapel of my dress. A wire was attached to this which was supposed to drop down the front of my dress on the inside, then drop below the hem-line so that he could connect it up as I appeared on stage. Suddenly the tiny little mike slipped from his hands and disappeared from view. Whether it was me trembling with stage-fright, or him being clumsy in his haste, is debatable, but the mike insisted on hiding in the folds of my dress somewhere around the waist. There was no time

for decorum; TV people work in fractions of seconds and I
was due on stage. Without further ado he stuck his hand
down my dress and fished out the stubborn mike. I don't
know who was more embarrassed, him or me. It was a
damn good job that I'd got a bra on! After the show he
made time to come and apologize but I told him it wasn't
necessary and we both ended up laughing about the
incident.

The programme I was on was a chat show type
presentation called Central Weekend. The topic of
discussion was mediums, and whether it was possible or
not to contact the dear departed. Doris Collins, being the
most celebrated and gifted of mediums, held centre stage.
I was given the seat next to Doris and then there were also
two male mediums and one female medium. Just before
the programme, the two male mediums and myself were
asked to do a consultation for three members of the
audience who wanted to contact someone who had
passed over. This consultation and the information that it
could or could not supply was to form the foundation of
the show. I was terrified.

I sat with the audience participator, Janeen, in an
attractive but small, claustrophobic dressing-room. This
may sound like an excuse but it was no place for me to
produce good results. I struggled through the session and
was far from pleased with the outcome. Oh, there were
one or two facts that I did manage to reveal about the
woman herself and her mother whom she wanted to
contact on the other side. But this was one reading that
was way below par for me and I certainly did not contact
her mother. As I waited to go on stage. I visualized the
forthcoming onslaught. I felt that I had failed miserably
and now I was about to be ridiculed, in public no less. I
had no sympathy for myself, knowing that I was stupid
and big-headed or pig-headed to think that I could work
on TV anyway. I was sure that the other two male
mediums had done so much better than I had. I even
hoped they had – anything was better than bringing the
whole profession into disrepute. Doris Collins herself saw
my dismay and attempted to cheer me up. She was easy to
talk to, very sincere and she gave me some good advice.

She told me not to experiment or try to make contact with the other side if I found my situation disturbing or distressing. I still went on stage expecting the worst, but knew that I had to face the music. The three women who had had consultations were now asked to comment on their experiences.

I listened anxiously as Andy Craige, the presenter, asked the first woman, Pauline, the following questions.

'Did you get anything out of that sitting?'

'No.'

'Nothing at all?'

'Just generalized. What anyone could have said to me. My next-door neighbour has said the same things.'

'Did you go in with an open mind though?'

'Yes definately.'

With that he turned his attention to Barbara.

'What about you Barbara?'

'I'm afraid I got nothing whatsoever out of the sitting. Just general things were said. For example, he said that he had ringing in his ears. Well, he should go see a doctor, not tell me.'

This statement made the audience laugh and me quake in my seat. Now it was my turn to be discussed, and Andy approached Janeen.

'But what about yourself Janeen?'

'Er ... I was disappointed, but I have to say, what Kris did say was something about my mum's back. Well, she did die of cancer of the spine and she did say, er, bones were brittling away. Well, her bones did because the cancer went all over her body. But basically I was disappointed.'

I nearly collapsed in front of the cameras. Doris Collins smiled at me, sensing my relief. From thereon I didn't care what was going to be thrown at me. Now I could cope – I would survive the evening. Not that I had much chance to say anything. Some very arrogant people in the audience made sure of that, although I did manage to voice my opinion on the subject of bereavement. On stage, when Doris was questioned, she was completely in control. The religious fanatics threw the usual quotes from the good book at her in order to discredit mediums in general. But

Doris could also quote the Bible and gave as good as she got, if not better.

The programme ended without conclusion which was exactly what I expected. Then we were all invited to stay on for refreshment and encouraged to continue our discussion. It was then that I met Bill Waddington, or 'Percy Sugden', of Coronation Street fame. A lot younger than he looks on TV and much more interesting, we talked for ages on psychic ability, and his knowledge on this subject was pretty good. He had a twinkle in his eye and a vice-like grip around my waist. This was a man who could be a lot of fun, not at all like the character he portrays on television.

Anna Soubry and Andy Craige, the presenters of the show, also found time to chat to both myself and my husband John. I have a strange feeling that John would have taken Anna home if it had been possible – she is certainly pretty and very talented with it. Andy Craige was charming and enjoyed pulling my leg about being nervous and losing the mike down my dress at the beginning of the show. All in all, it turned out to be a great night, with lively, friendly people at all levels. John and I returned home rather late but happy with the night's events.

I was approached by Central Television again in the summer of 1987, when they asked if I would be prepared to make some predictions for them. I said I'd be more than delighted. The very next day a young man called Tony Birkley arrived at my home to interview me, along with the sound, light and camera crew. They decided to do the recording in the front room because it's so much larger than the reading room. As soon as they had set up all their equipment I sat down at the table and prepared for the question I knew they were going to ask. (What was going to be the outcome of the next general election?) There had been a great deal of speculation on this subject. Everyone thought that Mrs Thatcher would lose, especially since the whole country appeared to be on the verge of a recession. The interviewer was most disappointed when I assured him that not only would Mrs Thatcher win, but she would win easily. I also told them that in 1989, Mrs Thatcher would personally select and groom her successor. It would be a young man, much younger than had ever been elected before. He had straight hair and glasses. This man would make *major* changes once he had the power and would go on to win another election for the Conservatives. These views were clearly frowned upon by the interviewer. It wasn't that Mr Birkley had any political preference, just that the general view, nation-wide, was a certain win for Labour. I was asked to confirm my prediction using percentages and stating seats that would be won, but it was obvious that they all thought the interview had been a waste of time. As the crew packed up to leave, I knew this recording was about to be shelved, and I was right about that too. However, the whole crew were friendly to the end and even managed to find some time to amuse my children, who thought it was great having a TV team in the house. Less than a month later, many were amazed to find that my predictions were almost one hundred per cent correct.

The success rate of the prophecies in that recording may not have been transmitted, but they weren't forgotten either. Central Television had much more confidence in me when I was given a slot during prime time viewing on the last day of 1990. I was proud to be asked to make predictions for many celebrities. When asked what 1991 had in store, I told them.

'There's going to be lots of changes, a hell of a lot of changes and Mr John Major will be responsible for much of this. He's certainly going to reign supreme for the next four years, there's no doubt about it and in fact, every day he's going to gain in popularity. People are going to like him, even the opposition are going to find that a lot of his ideas are workable. He has no intention of an immediate election. The feeling around John Major is 1992 will be the year that he will go forward and start to campaign again, and he will win, there's no doubt. With regard to Mrs Thatcher, it would be nice to say she was about to retire and see more of her grandchildren, but in truth I'm afraid she's coming back with a vengeance. I feel that she still has a lot of good work to do, but obviously in a lower position. Whatever she gets into, the nation will find out about. She will not give up politics even in the near future.'

I was then asked about British people involved in the Gulf War. 'Many will go back even though the problems aren't sorted out there. Most will return because they are faithful to their work and their bosses in that country, despite all the trauma around them. Some will need help with that trauma, but they will still return.'

The interviewer then asked about the Royal Family. I was very pleased to announce, 'Anyone expecting the Queen to abdicate is going to be bitterly disappointed. She's got many years to go yet and this is exactly what Charles and the Queen desire. So there's no abdication. Charles and Di's marriage is good. People keep reading about drifts and splits but in truth it's quite a good marriage. They will be seen to be working better and closer together this year.'

We then went on to talk about sports celebrities. 'Brian Clough is going to spend much more of his time involved in business and even invest in something in Nottingham. He will be just as popular off the field as he is on. He's certainly got a hell of a lot of business sense and I expect him to use it in the next few years. I do see him retiring after one more season. It's time for Gazza to read between the lines or read the small print. He's still got magic in his feet but I feel he's investing unwisely.'

I made many more predictions which Central decided not to use because of a limited amount of time, and they wanted to keep the New Year's Eve predictions as happy as possible. As they said, it's nice to start the year with something good to look forward to. I enjoyed my time with this outside broadcasting crew and it was extremely satisfying to know that this time they had enough faith in me and my predictions to transmit them.

I even found time to do constructive readings for the crew. Many of these very accurate predictions were confirmed at a later date. Mr John Major obliged by having his election on April 9th 1992, as predicted, and he won against all odds. Mrs Thatcher continues to support the government in a very active role. Many of the people involved in the Gulf War have indeed returned to their work and homes there. The Queen publicly announced in her Christmas speech that she had no intention of ever retiring. Mr Brian Clough has got more involved in business other than football. Have you seen all those adverts he does? And I've read that one of his sons has invested in a sports shop in Nottingham. As for his retirement, we'll just have to wait and see.

29 Who Do Voodoo

There is a tremendous amount of misconception about this weird and wonderful profession I'm involved in. I'm often accused of being a witch, a Satanist, or even a sorceress. It's true that I do believe in the essence of witchcraft, and that the ancient, authentic act of wicca should never be dismissed light-heartedly. I find myself drawn and sympathetic to the wretched females who became the innocent victims of over-zealous, vindictive defenders of certain Christian religions. The wicked and evil tortures these women endured at the hands of men who were supposedly virtuous, God-fearing church officials is enough to make any civilized, caring person cringe with pain and shame. Burning these women at the stake was often only the last of a multitude of barbaric atrocities they experienced. Many must have seen the burning as a blessed release from their long and inhumane suffering. However, that's another story, and one which should be told by someone more educated and experienced than I am. It remains for me to admit that all my efforts to defy gravity, engaging the use of a broomstick, failed miserably. I occasionally think of the money I could save though. I don't think there's a road tax, or flying tax for that matter, on broomsticks. Then there's the envious possibility of eliminating parking problems. However, the vision of shopping in the local Sainsburys, broomstick safely tucked in shopping trolley with the toilet rolls and cornflakes, always proves to be just a little too ridiculous.

It's often difficult to get through to some people that I am, first and foremost, a clairvoyant. I see, hear, more importantly, feel the emotions and problems of my clients.

I deal with the past, present and future as best as I can, although I must confess that the passage of time within a reading is often slightly distorted or even cryptic. This sort of confusion, with regard to my clairvoyant talent, was never made more apparent to me than the day a very intelligent and gracious Indian woman arrived at my Nottingham office for a consultation.

As she stepped in from the mist outside, I could feel the anger within her but I wasn't sure whether she was angry at the fog, the buses, being late, or maybe just at some personal problem she had. I told her to take off her damp coat and then I made her a cup of tea. I knew that we would have plenty of time to do her reading, for all of my clients who had booked in for the rest of that day had been kind enough to let me know that they wouldn't be able to keep their appointments, due to the fog.

It was difficult to put an age to this client. She had the classic Indian looks that frequently defy time. I guess she must have been in her late thirties or very early forties. Her attire was very English – a dark blue suit with a pale blue silk blouse. The matching handbag and shoes were obviously very expensive. The little make-up that she wore was just right for her dark skin. Her shiny straight black hair had been trimmed to a flattering shoulder length. This high calibre lady was as English as I, and yet it was easy to imagine her in the traditional costume of her country. She had managed beautifully to combine modern western style with the gracious and somewhat demure Indian culture.

The reading revealed that her husband had died suddenly, just over two years ago. This left her to bring up her two children alone, although they were both in boarding school. She had worked side by side with her husband and together they had built up a thriving business. However, since her husband's demise, she had encountered many problems. The biggest one was the dreaded mother-in-law, who had been brought over from India for the funeral. She had now decided to stay in England, at her dead son's and indeed my client's, house, keeping an ever-watchful eye on both my client and her son's business. Now many of us know how frustrating that can be, don't we? I always say that even a comedian wouldn't have found anything to joke about if he'd had my first mother-in-law. Anyway, this was only the first problem that she had to cope with. The next one was that for the first time in years, the business had started to lose money. The workforce, who had always been so diligent under her husband's supervision, now appeared to resent her. Those who she had once trusted now secretly plotted to undermine her. This was true, as the cards portrayed within this section were mainly swords, which are always bad news. Then there was the sixteenth card from the major arcana, *la maison de dieu*, more commonly known as the tower, or the house of God. No one has to be clairvoyant to interpret this card. The card itself depicts the ruin of property and men falling to their deaths. Within the picture are closed unyielding doors which deny sanctuary to all. Then the essence of hell looms from the very depths of the soil and foundations of the tower. Truly an unfortunate card, especially when it appears to represent the future, rather than the past.

This client wasn't imagining the disquiet around her. Not only did it exist, but it was growing out of all proportion. As if this wasn't enough for her to cope with, I then saw that she would soon have to go into hospital for a minor operation. She now confided that she had found a lump in her breast and was too scared to go to the doctor. I told her that, although the lump wasn't a malignant cancer, she still had to go. Only then would she have peace of mind. Just to please me, she promised to do so that very night.

One of her sons had created the next dilemma, and it was one that only time would solve. Since the death of his father, he had become lazy and disruptive at school. He'd had two warnings to pull his socks up – that sort of institute wouldn't tolerate a disobedient, sloppy student. I assured my client that her son was now over the worst and would soon be on the straight and narrow. All that she had to do was wait!

The next can of worms we opened was one of her own making, and as such quite a serious one. The psychic vision I now had of her was one that even frightened me. I saw her surrounded with the symbolic paraphernalia of witchcraft and voodoo. Instinctively I knew that she had been dabbling with the darker side of the occult. She hesitated a little when I described this view, then admitted that, because she had been inundated with so many complications over the past two years, she had contacted another clairvoyant for help. However this action had only served to add to the confusion in her life.

Apparently, this so-called clairvoyant had told her that she had been cursed at birth and this was why she was having such a bad time lately. Not only that, but the future held even more aggravation and the possibility of her son's death. If she wanted to be free of this 'curse' then the clairvoyant would have to burn a candle for her, and send up some sort of incantation. The trouble was that this would obviously cost a bit extra; fifty pounds extra to be precise! My client may have seemed ultra-modern, but deep inside strong ancient beliefs remained, so she coughed up the money in the hope that this women would be able to remove the curse. The clairvoyant then instructed her to return in seven days, whereupon she would prove that she had indeed lifted the curse. Guess what? You've got it! It appears that the curse was much stronger than she had anticipated. It would be necessary for the clairvoyant to travel to India in order to get to the roots of the spell and therein, destroy it. This flaming charlatan, for that's all she was unless you want to include the word thief, said that she had to collect eggs and herbs from where the client had been born. Then she would have to draw a mystic circle on the ground and chant some magic spells for up to seven hours. Then and only then would the evil be banished from the client's life. Well! I knew the client was in deep, but not that deep – the poor woman was out of her mind with worry. She had enough problems without being told she'd been cursed at birth.

My client then produced £500 from her bag and placed it carefully on the table in front of me. I almost stopped breathing! This was the deposit the other clairvoyant had demanded for services rendered. She would actually require £3,500 to complete the service. The thing that astonished me most was the fact that my client doubted this woman's credibility and yet was still prepared to part with such a large amount of money.

I was beginning to get angry, at the client and at the other clairvoyant. I had to ask why she had bothered to come and see me at all when she's obviously made up her mind to go ahead with this expensive farce. It turned out that she had confided in one of her friends, and a very good friend as it happens, about this (it's at this stage that my mouth goes out of gear) so-called clairvoyant. Her friend had insisted that she should ask for my advice before she paid the deposit. In fact, she had blackmailed her into seeing me, saying she would tell her mother-in-law what she was up to if she didn't produce evidence of her consultation with me within the week. So there she was, still slightly under protest, but now that the reading had proved so positive she was prepared to listen to what I'd got to say about her predicament.

First and foremost I advised her to put her money back into the bank and leave it there. Then I made it very clear that I'd never heard of this other woman, who was supposed to be an internationally well-known clairvoyant. I don't claim to know all practising psychics, but I do know most of them in this area. Then it was important for me to dispose of the supposed 'curse'. This was fairly easy. I simply asked her why the curse had taken so long to work. If the curse did exist, why had she had such a good life for so long? Her husband's death was not the delayed effect of some ancient curse sent to destroy her. As for the business, she had lost control because the very nature of the job required the attention of two bosses, both able to work inside and outside the factory. She would have to find a new partner if she wanted to get out of this rut. She was doing far too much on her own. Then I solemnly promised that her sons would come to no harm, and went on to discuss their somewhat favourable future.

Gradually, she began to believe me and decided there and then not to pay the £500 deposit – for the time being anyway. She was going to wait and see if my predictions proved valid. However, she told me straight, that if disaster struck again, she'd be returning to the other woman, charlatan or not, and paying the full price. It was then that she asked me if there was any way that she could get rid of her mother-in-law. I sympathized with her (don't we all?!) but there was little that I could do. That woman was determined to stay. I suggested that she should introduce her mother-in-law to as many elderly eligible males as possible. With luck, she would be rid of her in about three years. In the meantime, it was more important that she made new friends, even under those critical eyes. Developing a deaf ear would also prove advantageous if she was going to survive the next few years!

Six months later, this same client came to see me again. She hadn't paid to remove the curse. She had found another partner for the business, and although it was a little too soon to say that she was now making a profit, she actually felt that the workforce was once again with her. The partnership looked to be promising and even the mother-in-law approved of her choice. The children were still safe and sound. In fact, the son who had gone off the rails was now working hard. All in all it had been a good consultation. The reading had proved to be very successful and constructive. I was exceptionally pleased for my client, and chuffed with myself. The only fly in the ointment is that I still haven't had the opportunity to strangle the charlatan who posed as a clairvoyant. Women like her only succeed in making a lot of people miserable. Then true clairvoyants end up cleaning up the mess that's left. I also have this sneaky feeling that if I'd tried this shameful but lucrative scam, I would have been hung, drawn and quartered. Ah well! Such is life. Pass me the mop and bucket!

30 Black Magic

If I can get face to face with a client who has a problem, I can usually help. However, when the same person will only talk to me over the phone, then it's me who ends up with the problem. Take the time when a young woman, obviously in great distress, phoned to ask if I could help her if she had been involved with black magic. Then, before I could even answer, the phone went dead.

I worried all day about her, wondering what sort of mess she'd got herself into, hoping that she would call again soon. Later that night, just as I'd put my children to bed, she did. She was hysterical, frightened and crying. It was quite difficult to make out exactly what she was trying to tell me between such great, heaving, soul-destroying sobs. Then she screamed that she was going to kill herself and her two children rather than let her husband have them. My mind raced. I'm used to dealing with difficult situations, but this one was way out of my league. Someone must have put the right words into my mouth that night though. I managed to keep her talking; I had to keep her talking. I told her my name, then asked her what hers was. This seemed to panic her, so I quickly said it didn't matter, as long as she didn't mind me calling her love or duck. Then I asked her about her children – she had a girl and a boy. There was so much love for them in her voice; I couldn't believe that she would hurt them. This small-talk only took a few seconds, but it calmed her down enough to stop her crying. Now I asked her to slowly tell me why and how she had been dealing with black magic. Suddenly there was the sound of the pips – the money was about to run out. She said thank you for listening at the same time as I told her to phone again and reverse the charges. I didn't know if she'd heard me or not. So once again I was left to fret about someone who desperately needed help. As it happens, she phoned me four or five times over the next week. She said that just talking to me helped her to feel better. The whole sorry story was eventually revealed to me, a stage at a time, over the phone.

Apparently she had lived in Cornwall for about seven years. It was there that she had met and married her husband. They were quite well off, both of them having well paid jobs. After the birth of her first child, a daughter, she'd finished work and they were both happy for her to stay at home. Settling down to housewifely duties was, for her, a pleasure. He was very highly thought of at his place of work, so there were no financial problems. Then, just as she thought everything in the garden was growing and blooming perfectly, the proverbial happened. The depraved seeds of discontent and despair invaded not only her life but her very soul. Within this innocent and fertile environment, the weeds flourished and throttled all that was once pure and good around her.

Her husband had joined a small select club. Nothing wrong in that, or so she thought for a few weeks. Then he started to stay out later and later, until he wasn't coming home at all. Tina thought the obvious – that he was seeing another woman, and this caused a lot of violent arguments between them. After one particularly terrible fight he angrily told her that he hadn't got another woman. He then confessed to her that he had actually joined a group of satanists. For weeks Tina was in shock – this was something that she couldn't cope with. The whole idea went totally against her grain, as she was a practising Catholic. She couldn't understand, and she didn't want to understand, her husband's desire to join a bizarre cult. Then, adding insult to injury, he asked, then begged her, to attend at least one of their meetings. Using the age-old adages, 'you can't judge what you haven't tried', 'don't knock it till you've tried it', he succeeded in tearing the poor girl in two. She didn't want to lose the man she still loved, but she certainly didn't want to join this evil group. As the weeks passed he set her an ultimatum. Either she went to a couple of his meetings or the marriage was over. He then said that if she still didn't approve after she'd been at least twice, he too would give up the group. On these grounds, she followed him like a lamb to the slaughter. Soon she as as involved as he was. They even consented to conceiving another child at one of their sessions. The child, she was told, was certain to be born with great powers, which he would need later on in life. The only thing that was certain was that this pathic lady was about to have a mental breakdown. This, as it turned out, was her salvation.

In the hospital, away from the constant propaganda the group fed her, she began to see the light. I personally don't have much to do with any church or religion, but if it works for you then that, as far as I am concerned, is great. Tina now needed her belief to help her through what was going to be one hell of a fight. However, on this occasion, the church was tried and found wanting, in both love and understanding. Whilst the poor girl was in hospital she was approached by a man of the cloth who said he wanted to help her. She believed he could and would help, so she told him the entire story. This stupid man told her that she must return to her husband and get the pair of them back on the straight and narrow by following the Catholic faith. As soon as they had both renounced the satanic group, their sins would be forgiven and once again they would have the blessing of the Church. Now I don't know about you, but it's been my experience that husbands usually do as they bloody well please! Especially if they are interested or deeply involved in any sort of activity. Whether it's fishing, gambling, smoking, drinking, flirting or sleeping all day, they usually carry on regardless of what their partner thinks or feels, and it's only a wise or crafty woman who can get them to change their ways. So what chance did this poor girl have of getting her husband away from nothing short of an obsession? You got it in one – *none*!

Her only way out was to run, which was exactly what she did, taking her children with her. It must have been the hardest decision she's ever made in her life, and now she was at her wits' end, with nowhere to live and no money. Her voice lowered to a whisper when she told me that she often heard her husband's voice in the quiet of the night. She said that he still had the power to contact her through thought waves. He could still make her do things that she didn't want to do. He had started to command her to do 'things' to the children. God, I didn't want to know what 'things' – I didn't even want to think about it. I told her she had got to be strong and fight the voices. It would be so wrong for her to hurt the children.

I begged her to tell me where she was, but she was still afraid that I would call the police and the children would be taken away from her. Finally, she phoned one Sunday dinner-time to let me know that she had found a squat. I asked if the children were well and she said they were fine. However, her friend also had a child and although a little younger than Tina's daughter, this child's speech was far superior. She asked me if it was possible that her husband was controlling her daughter, restricting her speech from advancing. Even though they were miles apart, she still believed he had some sort of possession over her. Then the break came that I had been waiting for. She asked me if there was any sort of talisman which would help to protect her and the children from him. This was my chance to really help. I said that I would search through all my books and if there was such a charm, I would get it for her. But she would have to collect it, or at least tell me where she was. She said that she would phone again within the next two days.

I must have spent the next forty-eight hours scanning every book I had on satanism and witchcraft. I even got two friends of mine who know much more than I do about black magic to do some research for me. Between us we came up with one or two different charms. These were made with great precision and ritual. Cloth was used from one of my favourite dresses; this was to be the container. Seeds and herbs were collected, mixed and chanted over. Then a pure silver pentagon, surrounded by a silver circle, was also enclosed within the small black velvet bag. This was then sewn up tight to seal it. When I think about this now, I feel we must have looked like a scene from *Macbeth*. The three of us with our heads together – all we needed was a cauldron. Still, the job had to be done and it had to be done properly. We were not about to fob her off with some useless, ten-a-penny charm, and somewhere in the back of our minds we knew that we could only fight fire with fire. So to beat black magic we had to use magic. Magic works because it is willed to work and that night we had three heads all willing it to work, for the sake of a scared woman and two little kids.

When she called again, I told her that the charms were ready for her to personalize. She said that she would be round that very afternoon because she'd had two very restless nights. The voices had become more presistent and she couldn't get the charms fast enough if they were going to work. And they *were* going to work, because I had told her they would.

We decided that I should see Tina alone, as we didn't want to scare her away before we had the chance to help her. I cancelled any bookings that I could because I wanted to spend as much time with her as possible. Just as I'd given up hope of her coming, the doorbell rang. She stood there, a frightened little blonde who couldn't have weighed more than seven stone. The two kids were pale and quiet, but well wrapped up against the cold wind. She looked more like a sister than their mother, but you could see that she really cared for them. I invited her in for a cup of tea, but there was mistrust in her eyes – all she wanted was the charms. Then a little bit of natural magic happened. My own five-year-old daughter ran through the house like a lunatic, chasing a rather large black and white rabbit. Now this may not be normal in most people's homes, but in ours it was a regular day-to-day occurrence. Buggy (what else do you call a rabbit?) thought he was a dog, and spent most of his time in the front room under the radiogram. Maybe he liked music. Anyway, client or no client, he wanted to get back to his favourite spot under the gram, and no one, but no one, was going to stop him. Christine chased him around, almost knocking me over and trying to say she was sorry at the same time. She had had strict instructions not to disturb me. As she dodged backwards and forwards the two children started to laugh. This put everyone at ease. Buggy was eventually caught and the two children wanted to stroke him. They were now not in the least bit interested in what their mother had come for – Buggy was much more exciting so off they ran with my daughter. This gave me the chance to give Tina a cup of coffee and put her mind at rest. I think she still expected to find either the police or men in white coats in my front room. I suppose the last thing anyone would expect to find would be a large rabbit with a personality problem. I showed Tina the charms and told her exactly how they had been made and how they were expected to work. She hung onto my every word, not wanting to miss any detail. To put her mind at rest, I told her she didn't have to understand it, just trust it. This made her look a little happier.

As we watched the children play we talked about them. It was time for the girl to be in school and it was clear to me that she'd need elocution lessons. Tina agreed with me, but said it was her husband's fault. It was his way of getting at her because she was convinced that she was still under his spell. There was no point in arguing. I just had to let her know that my power was stronger than his, that I was capable of breaking any evil spell about her. I told her again and again that her husband would no longer be able to get to her. So now it was up to her to repair all the damage that had been done to them over the last five years.

The last thing she wanted was for social workers to decide that she wasn't a fit mother. So we had to set about proving how good a mother she was. She allowed me to contact a women's refuge and although pretty cramped, they said they would be pleased to help her. If I think about it now, it was the women at the refuge who actually broke the spell. No sooner had she got there than they helped her to get rented council accommodation. Then the little girl was placed in a special day school where she got the attention she needed in order to correct her speech. Child welfare were called in, but to her surprise, they were a great deal of help. She had never had anything to do with welfare people before and thought that they only came to take children away from bad parents.

Over the next nine months or so Tina often called to tell

me how she and the children were. Sometimes she would say how much she still missed her husband and how lonely she was. However, she liked the house, even if it wasn't as grand as the home she'd left in Cornwall. The children had settled down nicely, and no matter what her problems were, she was just happy to be away from satanism. Nothing, but nothing, could ever be as bad as the hell she'd gone through whilst she'd been with them and whilst escaping from them.

Tina still desperately needed her faith. She needed to belong to the Church, but was afraid of being rejected again or of being sent back to her husband.

I persuaded her to try the local Catholic church, and I said, 'If they don't want you, or try to send you back, try a different denomination. Someone, somewhere will want you and your children.'

She promised that she would try again and, as it happens, I now know that she kept that promise. She is now once again a good practising Catholic and happy to be so. As I always say, if religion works for you, then that's great. It doesn't matter which group, as long as it makes you feel good and responds to you with a loving caring nature. Don't worry about what the rest of the world thinks – just go for it. Tina found the love and understanding that she needed within her own denomination, even if it was at a different church.

31   John Rushworth Jellicoe

As you've heard me say, time and time again, I always class myself as a clairvoyant rather than a medium. However, like most people in this profession, I tend to dabble in anything to do with the occult. So, after reading a few books on mediumship and spiritualism, I decided to try to find out if I had one of those mysterious spirit guides, via the use of 'automatic writing'.

The books I read on automatic writing advised me to sit at a table in a darkened room at a quiet time of the day. The last requirement was especially difficult to acquire; ask any mother of four. I then needed a large piece of paper and an easy flowing pen. I assume those in spirit world get just as annoyed with dud pens as I do. After a few deep breathing exercises I was instructed to empty my mind. (Since this is something I do at the drop of a hat, I knew I had a head start!) After ten minutes meditation, I managed quite nicely to vacate my mind, and then I had to take up the pen and let it freely wander where it would, across the paper. To my complete amazement, I found that I had drawn about five miniature antique-type pictures of men, in very high, stiff-collared jackets. Now since I can't draw to save my life, I found this fascinating, especially as I had had my eyes closed all the time.

This completed my first experiment at automatic writing. I was both pleased and intrigued by the result. In fact, I was hooked, and found myself returning to the table, pen in hand, as often as circumstances would allow. After a few sessions I started to get words and a name. I kept getting, in rather scratchy, spidery writing, *'I'm not to blame, communications, communications.'*

Well, I thought that spirit world was having a go at me,

trying to tell me that the bad line we had was all my fault. I vaguely recall accepting the blame, but persevered anyway. It was then that I was rewarded with the name, in signature form, of J.R. Jellicoe. A lot of you probably know all about this man. What's more, you're liable to think that I must be awfully thick, because I assure you that I could not, at that time, produce any information on this man. In fact, I thought it was quite a silly name and came to the conclusion that I must have spelt it wrong.

As the sessions progressed, the writing became easier, quicker and clearer. Soon it wasn't just my hand that was being taken over. My entire body became the container for the mind of someone in spirit. I guess you could say that I was possessed. I'd sit quietly for about five minutes, then allow myself to be drawn into the setting that usually started out as a mental picture or thought. Almost as if I was exploring my own brain. Then my arms felt heavy, the right arm and shoulder feeling particularly painful, and the sensation of coarse cloth was all about my skin, especially around my wrist. The pen which had previously dangled lazily from my fingers now snapped to an uncomfortable upright position, forcing me to write in an awkward manner. On many occasions I had the distinct impression that there was a large invisible dog leaning lightly against my leg. The name Jellicoe became stronger and stronger, and my ignorance irritated me, so I went to the library and did some research. For those of you like me, whose education leaves a lot to be desired, especially when it comes to historical facts, I'll tell you all that I now know about the earthly exploits and achievements of this very powerful and intriguing man.

John Rushworth Jellicoe, the son of a sea captain, was born in Southampton in 1859. In his early twenties he served in the Egyptian war of 1882, somehow managing to survive a terrible collision between HMS *Victoria* and HMS *Camperdown*. During the First World War he was appointed Commander-in-Chief of the Grand Fleet and his flagship was the *Iron Duke*. He was in command at the battle of Jutland, and became First Sea Lord in 1916. His promotion to Admiral of the fleet came in 1919 and he ended up as the governor of New Zealand in 1920. A very important man indeed. I felt extremely honoured that this incredible man would have anything to do with a simple mortal such as myself. On discovering these facts I came to the conclusion that the coarse cloth I so frequently felt was in fact his navy uniform. Also, he may have been left-handed or just written in an awkward manner. This would explain the difficulty I had when holding the pen during the automatic writing sessions. I also believe that, because of the miniature pictures I drew, he had an artistic streak in him. He must have liked dogs, but so far I've found no record of him having a large dog as a constant companion.

I feel privileged to have a sailor as a spirit guide. A navy man with a name and lots of fascinating history to back him up. I still contact Mr Jellicoe, or John as I have come to call him, and he actually helps me sometimes with my clients when I'm working. I never feel sad when he's with me, so I know he's happy enough and not some lost spirit destined to wander in the land of limbo for eternity. In fact, he's still a bit of a lad, and I blame him for a very interesting spirit picture that mysteriously appeared on the wall in my very own kitchen in the autumn of 1991.

I'd finally got the builders in to enlarge my unbelievably small, poorly planned kitchen. This entailed taking down two walls and one of those separated the kitchen from the living-room. Then they had to re-erect the dividing wall further back into the living-room. The end result left me with a slightly smaller front room but a much bigger kitchen. The builders were very efficient – the walls went down on Friday, were re-erected on Saturday and on Sunday they finished all the plumbing, electrics and plastering. However, I was warned that the plaster could take up to three or four days to dry, especially since it was cold and damp outside. They knew I was in a hurry to start painting and decorating but advised me against this until it was all completely dry.

The following day was a Monday and I was glad to get the children off to school so that I could start to clean up as much as possible. I ignored the kitchen most of the day and concentrated on hoovering and dusting the front room, passage, stairs and bedrooms. Plaster dust was everywhere. I didn't exactly relish the thought of cleaning the kitchen, but it had to be done, and by the time my husband got home, it was almost presentable, as long as you didn't look at the walls.

On Tuesday night at about nine o'clock I was leaning against the kitchen sink, wondering if I would ever get straight, and there on the damp plastered wall, to my utter amazement, I saw a picture of my dog. I couldn't believe it and I thought for a minute I was hallucinating. I shouted John into the kitchen and even as we stood there, the picture became stronger, more solid.

As luck would have it, there was a film in my camera, so I even got our own dog to pose with the picture. It was impossible for the picture to have been done by the builders, plasterers or even the children. No one could have known how that plaster would have dried, and that's what it was – just wet and dry plaster. It was impossible for any human to produce such a picture. The next day I was very disappointed to find the picture had disappeared overnight. However I did have a permanent reminder as the photographs came out quite well.

The story doesn't end there though. Just after Christmas we went to Horncastle to visit my mother and my daughter, Sarah. I showed them the photos and Sarah was especially interested because when she was at home, the dog was more hers than anyone's. She suddenly declared that the dog on the wall, or the spirit picture, was wearing her neck chain. We all looked a little closer at the photos and we had to agree it certainly looked like the chain around Sarah's neck. Apparently she wears this necklace all the time. It is a little unusual as the name Sarah is stamped out in gold and the letters actually form part of the chain. The mystery remains. I personally blame J.R. Jellicoe, not that I mind, but next time he feels like painting I hope he manages to make it more permanent, and puts it in a place where I can at least frame it.

32   John Adam and Ida

One morning in the early spring of 1979 I awoke in great pain in a hospital bed. Two days previously, during an emergency operation, the surgeon had removed a burst fallopian tube which, sadly, had held a sixteen week old baby. This kind, patient doctor was now trying to tell me exactly what they'd done. Apparently there was nothing they could have done for the baby, and in fact, they said I was lucky to be alive myself.

These type of pregnancies are called ectopic pregnancies and are often very dangerous, sometimes even fatal. During the operation the surgeon had also discovered that the ovary and tubes on the other side were useless, so technically I was now sterile. I accepted their verdict and considered myself lucky to have three smashing little girls. However, the psychic side of my brain rejected the doctor's diagnosis. Whilst I slept, I frequently received a small trailer-type scene. You know, like the ones you get at the beginning of a film to advertise forthcoming attractions. The dream was always the same. First of all, I would see myself in an all-too-familiar lounge bar. Then a young athletic man, at least six feet two inches tall, would walk past me. He wore jeans and a white T-shirt, his arms tanned and strong. He had fair hair that was cropped short, and as he turned towards me, I could see his big blue eyes and a smile that would break any girl's heart. Then he would casually say, 'Do you want a drink Mum?'

That's right, this was my son, but surely this psychic vision had to be wrong. The doctors had told me that conceiving another child was now impossible. So why? Why was this clipping or trailer played like a video recording night after night for three solid years?

How wrong those doctors were proved to be three years later. And how pleased I was, once I'd got over the initial shock. After all, I was getting a bit long in the tooth for having children. I went on to give birth to my one and only boy. What else could it have been? I named him John after his dad and grandad. Then, because he was my first boy, I named him after the first man in the garden of Eden. Adam. My own little John Adam. John was born veiled or shrouded. This actually means that he was born with a thin film of skin or membrane over his face. In fact, it was so thick that at first you couldn't see his little face and of course he was having difficulty in breathing. But the marvellous nursing staff knew just what to do and John was soon breathing normally.

Being born veiled is supposed to be lucky, and means that the child will never drown. In years gone by, many a ship's captain would buy a child's veil, then have it framed and mounted in their cabin. Some would seal the veil in a small casket in order to protect it from the light. It was said that a ship with a child's veil on board would never flounder nor sink.

Anyway, enough of these old wives' tales, although if I don't believe them, who will? Let's get on with the story. John Adam was a perfectly normal child, well loved and adored by us all. None of us were prepared for the terrifying episodes that were to follow.

When John Adams was about three months old, I moved him back into my room. He'd been a bit grizzly with teething and I didn't want him to disturb my two older girls, who were studying hard for exams. I'd put his cot at the side of my bed so that I could comfort him through the night. I often used to sleep with my hand through the bars of the cot and hold his tiny little hand.

That morning, at about 2.45, I was almost thrown out of bed. I thought, for a moment, that my husband had gone mad, but he was still fast asleep. I must have been dreaming. Once again as my head hit the pillow, I was pulled into an upright position. I actually felt my nightie tighten around my shoulders and then the fabric bit into my skin. Now I was wide awake and totally confused. Whilst trying to decide if I was going crazy or not, I automatically put my hand into the cot to check on the baby. I expected to find the usual – a warm hairy head, or a chest moving up and down in the dark, or maybe a tiny hand eager to hold my finger. This was not to be. My hand felt a damp, plastic-type face, like that of a wet doll. Now both hands were in the cot searching frantically for the warm moving body of the baby in the dark. I must have screamed and put the light on at the same time. My husband woke immediately. Within a split second he'd snatched the limp blue-black child from the cot and instinctively started to do mouth to mouth resuscitation. I just stood there uselessly, backing up to the wall. John could see that I was in shock, and he shouted at me to phone for the ambulance. That ambulance seemed to take forever, though it couldn't have been more than about five minutes. John continued to do mouth to mouth and heart massage until the ambulance men arrived. Then, just as they were about to put an oxygen mask over baby John's tiny blue face, his eyes opened. He coughed and choked, vomiting up a watery substance. He snatched air into his lungs with a frightening growling sound, like that of a wild animal caught in a trap. The ambulance man gently but firmly took the child from my husband's trembling arms and put the oxygen mask over the baby's face. Then we all raced off to the hospital. We were only at the hospital for about ten minutes when John Adam, my precious baby, was fast alseep and oblivious to the concern of all around him. His breathing had returned to normal and his tiny face, although still very pale, was relaxed and calm. My own heart-beat slowed down when a kind nurse offered me a cup of tea. The doctors decided to keep John Adam in hospital for a few days, just for observation, so I made arrangements to stay with him. My poor husband returned home when he was sure that baby John was out of danger and sent the older children to school. Every possible test was done on John Adam, but they couldn't find any apparent reason for him to stop breathing. So we were sent home with a letter for our doctor.

I know that we were not supposed to open that letter, but John said he had a right to know what had happened.

So unceremoniously, the letter was ripped open. All it said was 'Near miss cot death'. From that day on, we watched baby John like hawks. John's cot was permanently at the side of our bed, and we took it in turns to sleep or catnap, with a hand on his chest. The weeks passed and even we were beginning to think that we'd become slightly neurotic. Then the unthinkable happened. A repeat performance, almost identical to the last attack, and John was rushed to the hospital again. Then just as before, he recovered with little or no medication.

Baby John had five attacks in ten months, leaving my husband and myself almost out of our minds with worry, and exhausted through lack of sleep. But we still had our baby and that made it all worthwhile. There was no explanation as to the cause of the attacks and the doctors at the hospital said that we were very lucky to catch him every time. I don't think they realized that he was being watched twenty-four hours a day, in and out of hospital.

It was after the third attack, as my husband and I were resting in bed, that I asked him if he'd noticed anything unusual or strange about the house, especially when baby John was ill. He said he had, but he would prefer me to say what I'd sensed first as he felt a little uncomfortable with his own thoughts and ideas. It was then that I carefully told him that I could smell his mother, who had passed on two years before baby John had even been conceived. Not that John's mum ever used strong perfume, but she was a nurse and always had that slightly antiseptic smell about her. This was the odour that seemed to fill the house, before, during and just after the baby's attacks. The aroma itself was ten times stronger than I remembered from Ida, but it was definitely recognizable as hers. John admitted that he too had been aware of the odour and also that for him it was easily identifiable as that of his beloved mother's.

We both believe that it was Ida who woke us up the night that John Adam had his first attack. Also that it was Ida who so forcefully pulled me from my bed that night, knowing that even if I was only half awake, I would still check on the baby. She never had to use such force again but the spirit and the perfume of Ida continued to warn us if baby John was in any danger for the next year. We came to trust and rely on the familiar smell of Ida's perfume. Using it as an early warning alarm, it put us all on red alert for any forthcoming health problems. As soon as her aroma drifted around the house, we knew that we would be phoning for a doctor within the next twenty-four hours. It was as if she was constantly watching over him. This now makes me wonder if maybe she didn't quite trust me to do the job properly! I know that John Adam wouldn't be alive today if Ida hadn't been his guardian angel.

Ida's visits and warnings became fewer and weaker as her grandson John grew stronger. However, there are still times that I feel her presence about me. She no longer produces quite the same dramatic effect, but she sure lets me know she's there if I ignore her! It's strange really, because she always said that when she retired she was going to live with me, whether I wanted her or not. She even chose her room, which is now my consultation room, and I think I have little choice but to share it with her.

On many occasions, almost as soon as I start a reading, Ida will dim the lights if my client is a nurse. Once she actually blew the bulb because one of her nursing friends had turned up for a reading. So you see, I haven't lost Ida, because she's done exactly what she said she was going to do. She came to stay with me and very glad of her we are. She's welcome to stay as long as she likes. Although I wouldn't like to think that we were stopping her from resting in peace, or doing whatever you are supposed to do once you've passed over to the other side. Mind you, come to think of it, no one ever told Ida what to do – at times she was quite bloody-minded. So I guess she is doing exactly as she wants to. As usual!

33   Religion

Personal religious beliefs have no bearing on clairvoyance or psychic power at all. You can be psychic no matter which religion, cult or country you belong to. However, it is important that you understand how I feel about religion for two reasons. Firstly, only with this information will you have a complete picture of me and how my mind works. The second reason that I lay open my heart and thoughts to you on this very personal matter, is because there are an awful lot of people out there who think and feel as I do. I refer to people who find most religions complicated and confusing. There is no luxury of a church, chapel or mosque for us, nor the safety of a large gathering of like-minded people. Neither can we admit our sins and cleanse our souls at the feet of the almighty in order to free ourself from any blame or condemnation. We believe that we are responsible for our own actions on this earth so we blame no God for man's many misdeeds or the wars fought in the name of one religious cult or another. Our needs are few and the very nature of our beliefs sets us quietly and anonymously in the background. We understand the need for many to belong but we have no desire to do so ourselves. I too would like to believe in a particular faith. However, for people like me, religion is nothing more than a likeable child's fairy story. Personally, my clients are my religion. Through them I feel pain, pity, sympathy, pride, worry and worship. I need no church, just the sky above me and the love that surrounds me.

As a child I found my God on Bluebell bank. It was there that my father encouraged me to look at life, enjoy it and try to understand it. I remember walking over seven or eight fields to get to the bank from my home. The walk used to take us past hedgerows where we'd gather blackberries for Mum's pies or thick vinegar. Then we would pour this vinegar over the golden light Yorkshire puddings that accompanied our Sunday dinner.

Often those same hedgerows would provide us with hedge-roses and catkins, pussy-willow and dog-daisies. We would collect whatever was in season and Mum would duly put them in vases. Even if she didn't particularly like what we'd gathered or the vast amount of it, it had been gathered with love and as such would be treated with respect.

Most of the time with my father at my side, and always with my old dog, we would continue our journey past the hedges and over the fields to reach the bank where so few people ever bothered to visit. This made the bank special to me; you could say that this was indeed my church. It was quiet there, away from the other children. I would lie in the deep untrodden grass and enjoy the sun and the wind upon my face. As the name suggests, in late April and early May, the bank was ablaze with bluebells, and I called them all my own. I used to spend hours picking them, most of them true blue, but if you knew where to look, there were white, purple or even pink ones.

Dad and I would listen for the first cuckoo and try to spot it, though I don't think we ever did. Sometimes we would have serious talks on how the world could be made a better place to live in. More often than not though, there would be no need to talk, each of us understanding the other's needs. When we stood on Bluebell bank we could see for miles. The view was breathtaking with its banks and brooks, its fields and trees. Dad used to say, 'Enjoy it now, my lass, cos it won't be there long. Soon all that you see will be houses, factories and roads.'

How right he was. I went back to the bank about fifteen years ago. Even then I could see the houses and roads creeping closer and closer, threatening to engulf my precious childhood sanctuary. I took my two girls there. I felt I needed them to meet my God, in my church, before it disappeared altogether. Despite the fact that the houses were getting nearer, the bank remained as deserted as before. It was obvious from the height of the grass that no one had been there in years. My church remained intact and to this day, somehow, still exists, even though there are houses less than a field away. I must pay another visit soon and introduce my two younger children to the magic of my childhood.

I now feel that I have introduced you to my God, in my church. I wonder how you feel about a woman who needs neither bricks nor mortar, Bible nor prayer book, parson nor priest, church nor chapel. As I've stated before, there is nothing wrong in needing to belong to or believe in any particular church or religion. If it makes you feel good and if it's where you find your God, then that's all that matters. May you continue to be happy and content with your faith for the rest of your life. As my father used to say, 'Every man has his own god, and no man has the right to destroy that god.'

We have to allow people to worship who or what they desire, in the same way that we permit them to eat what they need. Just because it's a different culture or religion, a different strange unknown God, doesn't make them wrong and us right, just plain different. As long as beliefs don't cause pain or suffering to others, we should leave each other to get on with it. Let's face it, life would be very boring if we were all the same. I wonder what we'd fight over then?

Over the years I've read cards for many, many people. Young and old, male and female. Rich and poor, happy and sad, all races and religions. Many have tried to convert me to their own particular religion. Some say that I am evil and that one day their God will punish me for using my power, such as it is. Others have told me that my gift will be taken away from me because I charge for a consultation. Yet still they come when they are alone, sad, afraid or just plain curious. They turn up on my doorstep in the hope that I can and will help. I like to think that I have in fact helped many of them to sort out their lives.

I know that I have never, ever intentionally hurt or worried any of my clients. My aim in life is to improve the lives of others in some way, shape or form. Oh, I know that I've made mistakes and there's been many a time when I've bitten off more than I could chew. This book, at times, has proved to be more than a mouthful, but you've just got to keep chomping, especially when you hit the tough bits.

I may have steered many of my clients away from any impending disasters but they in turn have taught me so many things. Things that Mum and Dad tried to protect me from, because they weren't nice to know or they might have given me nightmares. My sheltered childhood was wonderful and every child should have one. However, finding out how the other half lives was alarming, distressing and frightening. I thought that everyone had a life as simple and uncomplicated as mine. My clients soon put me right on that account. They taught me to listen and love in a very different way to that which I'd known. They taught me to appreciate what I had and who I was. They gave me pain when I couldn't help and sorrow when I didn't try. Some would boost my confidence, whilst others would cruelly put me down. All these lessons I had to learn and learn fast, if I was going to stay in this caring profession and not break under the strain, as many do. Sadly too many budding psychics become totally involved in either the lives of their clients, or the evil side of the occult. Even the best of us can and do lose our way. Many pay a very high price when their approach to psychic power is clouded with ignorance and greed. There's a very fine dividing line between being psychic and psychotic. I often meet people who have crossed this line and lost all their powers of reason. The spirit they once treasured, along with their psychic ability, is trapped in a cage of self-pity or, worse still, they suffer from delusions of grandeur. These people cannot help themselves, let alone anyone else. They set themselves up as mediums and clairvoyants, then bring about more pain and problems for the client than they previously had. Fortunately, I've had, and still do have, many friends who have helped me to keep my feet on the ground, even when my head is in the clouds. So, my friend, beware. If you do need the help of a psychic, look for one that is at least sane. And if you are a budding clairvoyant or medium, don't lose track of reality. For it's far too easy to do just that in this crazy, mind-boggling profession.